OCR

D0965821

Our Stories of Miscarriage

Our Stories of Miscarriage

Healing with Words

Edited by Rachel Faldet
and Karen Fitton

Fairview Press
Minneapolis

Published by Fairview Press, 2450 Riverside Avenue South, Minneapolis, MN 55454.

Library of Congress Cataloging-in-Publication Data
Our stories of miscarriage : healing with words / edited by Rachel Faldet and Karen Fitton

       p. cm.
       Includes bibliographical references.
       ISBN 1-57749-033-9 (pbk.)
       1. Miscarriage—Psychological aspects.   I. Faldet, Rachel, 1956–.
II. Fitton, Karen, 1949–.
RG648.084   1997
618.3'92'019—dc20   96–35348

First Printing: April 1997
Printed in the United States of America
01 00 99 98 97   7 6 5 4 3 2 1

Cover design: Rich Rossiter

Publisher's Note: The publications of Fairview Press, including *Our Stories of Miscarriage*, do not necessarily reflect the philosophy of Fairview Hospital and Healthcare Services or their treatment programs.

For a free catalog, call toll-free 1–800–544–8207.

Acknowledgments for previously published work:
"Pipik" by Susan J. Berkson first appeared in *Minnesota Women's Press*, January 25, 1995; reprinted by permission of Susan J. Berkson and *Minnesota Women's Press*. Portions of "Branden and Kevin" by LaDawna Lawton first appeared in *Sacramento Baby Resource Guide* (1994); reprinted by permission of LaDawna Lawton and *Sacramento Baby Resource Guide*. "For the Child" by Evelyn Fielding first appeared in *Collection of Poems for the Unknown Child* (Legacy Press, 1993); reprinted by permission of Evelyn Fielding and Legacy Press. "Grey Flowers" and "Pattern" by Evelyn Fielding first appeared in *Blueberry Pie* (Same Name Press, 1992); reprinted by permission of Evelyn Fielding and Same Name Press. "Tribe" by Roseann Lloyd first appeared in *Tap Dancing for Big Mom* (New Rivers Press,1986); reprinted by permission of Roseann Lloyd and New Rivers Press. "Second Baby, Maybe" by Jorie Miller first appeared in *Rag Mag* 13, no. 1; reprinted by permission of Jorie Miller and *Rag Mag*. "Ritual for a Miscarriage" by Kelly Winters first appeared in *Iowa Woman*, Summer 1994; reprinted by permission of Kelly Winters and *Iowa Woman*.

To David and Robert

CONTENTS

FOREWORD

Fran Rybarik, R.N., M.P.H.

It is a deep honor to be part of this anthology of stories about miscarriage. When Karen Fitton and Rachel Faldet first talked about their idea for this book and asked me to help them contact parents who had experienced miscarriages, I sensed their excitement and shared their vision.

As the director of Bereavement Services/RTS (formerly Resolve Through Sharing), I work primarily with health care professionals. Over eleven thousand professionals from many health disciplines have completed RTS training because they have wanted to improve the care that is provided to families that experience pregnancy and perinatal losses.

Sharing Karen and Rachel's vision, I told professionals and grieving parents who called me with questions concerning miscarriage about the opportunity to be part of this book. In addition, I asked Rachel and Karen to provide abstracts describing their project for an international bereavement conference that RTS hosted in Chicago, Illinois in the fall of 1995. I wondered how it would all turn out. Now the book is a reality, and I am proud to be part of it—a few stitches around the edge of a beautiful quilt.

Many parents who have experienced miscarriages call our office. They are often searching for reasons why the miscarriage occurred, feeling lonely and isolated, wondering if their dreams in the night and feelings in the day mean they are going crazy, grieving differently than their partners or other family members, and wondering how long their profound sadness will last. They seek a connection with others who have had similar experiences—clinically, personally, and emotionally. Sharing feelings and thoughts about miscarriage and grief is often healing.

When pregnancy ends in a miscarriage, it is a crisis within a crisis. The whole person is affected—physically, emotionally, socially, and spiritually.

Hormonal changes of early pregnancy require the body to use much energy to adapt to a new state of physical equilibrium. With miscarriage, the body needs even more energy to readjust hormonal levels once more. There are emotional effects from adjusting to the idea of being pregnant, and from preparing to become a new parent or a parent again. Suddenly it all ends. Many questions arise: "Why me? Why my baby? What did I do wrong?"

It may be hard for parents who've lost a child through miscarriage to go to family gatherings or other social events, especially if other family members or friends are pregnant. Going to the grocery store and seeing babies or pregnant women can be devastating. The sense of aloneness or isolation can be very deep.

Miscarriage also often brings with it a spiritual crisis. Core beliefs suddenly come into question. Babies aren't supposed to die; everyone else gets pregnant and has babies; this isn't how life should be. Everything a person believes about life and love feels threatened.

The writings in *Our Stories of Miscarriage* identify and clarify many of these primary, as well as many secondary, issues. The essays, journal entries, and poems validate research showing that over seventy percent of women perceive their miscarriages as the loss of a baby. Whether parents perceive their miscarriage as the loss of a baby or the loss of a pregnancy, there are also secondary losses for them to consider.

Parents will confront the loss of control (especially if the cause of the miscarriage remains unknown), perhaps the loss of creation or fertility, and the loss of hope for the baby and for themselves. Some may mourn the lost opportunity of becoming a parent and the lost experience of a developmental stage in adulthood—described by contributor Jean Streufert Patrick in her essay as "joining the league of women."

Miscarriage is a life-marker event that bereaved parents will never completely forget. The grieving parents must travel the journey of grief and work very hard to integrate this experience and this loss into their lives. Some people do this in creative ways, like writing, and find it very healing.

Our Stories of Miscarriage will touch your heart. The book is a unique collection of thoughts and feelings of people who have experienced miscarriages. It provides a much-needed emotional connection for grieving parents. Through its powerful stories, it also provides a sense of understanding for family, friends, and professionals who are looking for ways to support someone on their journey of grief after a miscarriage.

The voices of bereaved parents tell of their sorrow and strength, anger and fear, and healing and hope. The contributors to this literary quilt of essays, journal entries, and poems are sharing their memories of their pregnancies and unborn children. By sharing, they help all of us who read their words to understand and acknowledge the wide variety of responses to the grief of early pregnancy loss. By remembering and by writing, they are able to live and grow through the parenting and bereavement experience called miscarriage.

ACKNOWLEDGMENTS

Putting this book together has been like making a friendship quilt: many hands and hearts contributed pieces to the whole.

Like friendship quilts, so often given to women in the nineteenth century who were leaving a familiar home for the unknown frontier, this quilt of words was made for a particular circumstance. Like those quilts, whose blocks of calico patchwork, appliquéd flowers, or embroidered silks were often inscribed with words of remembrance, this book is meant to be a work of comfort and hope.

Our quilt pieces have come from people near and far, most of them unknown to each other and, many times, initially unknown to us. Some of these quilt pieces, like the writings, are brightly visible. Others, like good advice, have been subtly stitched in with invisible thread.

As seamstresses who have put the pieces together, we have many to thank.

We thank those who spread the word that we wanted to collect writings on miscarriage, those who sent their writings, those who said this book was needed, those who discussed ideas with us as the manuscript took shape, those who cared for our children while we worked, those who helped with computer matters, those who gave us practical guidance on the world of books, and those who brought our project to press.

In particular, we thank the contributors. Your writings are the quilt blocks, the varied fabrics of shared sorrow and warmth.

We thank Paul Andersen, Sarah Andersen, Kathi Appelt, Nancy Barry, Judy Boese, Susanna Bullock, David Faldet, Robert Fitton, Cathi Lammert, Elizabeth Levang, Deborah Lischwe, Karen Murphy, Audrey Osofsky, Beth Hoven Rotto, Fran Rybarik, Robert Schultz, Timothy Twito, and Mary Jane White. Your stitches have helped secure the quilt blocks in place and guided us in finding their overall pattern.

We thank the Faculty Development and Research Committee at Luther College, which gave the project some financial assistance. You understood that quilters need pin money for supplies.

And, finally, we thank Julie Smith, Lane Stiles, and Ed Wedman of Fairview Press for putting the binding on our quilt of words and sending it out into the world.

INTRODUCTION

Rachel Faldet

It is a late night, nearly midnight, and my two daughters are sleeping. I can hear Elizabeth's restless breathing as she has a dream she will not remember in the morning. She is nine. I can't hear Pearl even though her crib is close by. I know the rhythms of her night and she won't cry for me until daylight. She is two years old. I had two miscarriages after Elizabeth was born and I had nearly given up hope of having another baby.

I had nearly given up hope because I couldn't bear the thought of losing another child. Having a miscarriage one year and another the next made me continually sad, although I carried on in my public life, doing what I always did—teaching writing, being a freelance writer and editor, and taking care of Elizabeth. I cried only at home, wanting to be a mother of a living child again.

My first miscarriage in late May of 1991 didn't surprise me. I had bleeding very early on and that didn't seem right, as I'd had none when I was pregnant with Elizabeth. I hoped the pregnancy would continue but, in a way, hoped it would end as the bleeding seemed a sign of a baby who could never be normal. An ultrasound at ten weeks showed the baby had died at eight weeks. My doctor and I decided I should have a dilatation and curettage (D&C).

I remember being wheeled into the operating room and crying uncontrollably once I got there. I'd known for about a week that the baby was dead, but part of me was hoping my doctor would say the baby was alive. I was frightened of the D&C, although I knew I had to go through with it. My husband and I had planned a June trip to see friends back in the places we'd lived in Idaho and Washington. I couldn't wait for my body to miscarry the baby naturally because we planned to leave in a few days and I needed to start to heal.

After the D&C, I was put in an outpatient room with only a curtain shielding me from other people recovering from surgical procedures. I tried not to cry because I didn't want anyone to hear me, but I couldn't help it. I cried and slept restlessly for about eight hours, and then went home. I cried and slept for three days. After that, David, Elizabeth, and I left Iowa for a month. I never told my Decorah friends about my miscarriage and scarcely told my family. I didn't want to think about it; I didn't want to face it. Since no one except my parents and David's parents knew I was pregnant, the miscarriage wasn't something I could talk about unless I brought it up. I didn't even tell many of the friends we'd driven halfway across the country to see.

The next time I became pregnant—in November of that same year—I was scared I would have another miscarriage. I felt unlucky, but I wasn't having any spotting or bleeding as with the miscarried pregnancy. Even though I tried to remain neutral, burying my emotions, I was surprised when I started bleeding at twelve weeks. Everything up to that point had seemed so right.

I was talking on the phone to a man I didn't even know. He had gotten our names from someone at an auction where we'd bought an antique wardrobe and wanted to buy it from us. As I was telling him it wasn't for sale, I felt a gush of warm blood and thought I was going to faint. I hung up the phone. The room seemed full of flashing lights. I went to the bathroom and saw the blood. I screamed and ran to the phone to call my mother. She hadn't even known I was pregnant. I went to bed and cried and slept. When I was awake, my very existence seemed hazy, as though I were looking down at a curled-up body covered with quilts. My mother and my cousin took turns watching over me that day.

This time I had nowhere to go—no friends to visit out West— so my doctor thought I should just wait to let my body miscarry the child. I waited two weeks, not wanting to leave the house in case blood came pouring out of me. I tried to appear normal and was glad I was only teaching a class that met once a week. David taught it for me. Finally, the blood came and with it came dangerous hemorrhaging. I had to go to the hospital at midnight for an emergency D&C.

This time, in February of 1992, I couldn't hide the fact that something traumatic had happened. I cried for hours at a time. I couldn't get out of bed to do anything for nearly a week. I had no interest in my daily life. I couldn't trust myself to go out in public as I was afraid I would cry for no apparent reason. Devastated, I neither wanted to—nor could—put on a facade of happiness and normalcy. I was the mother of two children who had died.

So I told people. I wrote letters from bed to my good friends in Decorah and around the country. I told Elizabeth. She was five and had known I had gone to the hospital in the middle of the night. She was afraid that I was going to die. She told her preschool teachers, the children's librarian at the public library, and our neighbors. "Mommy had a very tiny baby who died," she'd say. "She's had two tiny babies who died. But I didn't die."

I grieved for both of the miscarried babies. For the next few months, I cried often. I'd be making supper and I'd start crying. I'd see a pregnant woman downtown and I'd have to hold back my tears. I couldn't talk to a Decorah friend who was pregnant because seeing her made me feel sadder. I felt guilty about this, but my emotions were so tangled that I couldn't even explain my silence to her. As her pregnancy advanced, I grew more silent. Her baby was due the same week in September as my second miscarried child had been due. My sister in Atlanta, Georgia had had a baby the month and year that my first miscarried child was due. These two little girls, Sophie and Kate, became reminders of the two babies I had lost.

My grief was very lonely. Miscarriage happens in about twenty percent of all pregnancies, but that gave me only an abstract sort of comfort. For a while it was a statistic to which I could only attach two other names. Where were all these other women who'd had miscarriages? What had happened to them and how did they cope? Had they felt hollow, like me, as if they were ghosts of themselves looking at the world with little enthusiasm? Often it seemed I was the only person anywhere trying to cope with unfamiliar, confusing feelings of loss and grief. A quiet, lonesome sadness accompanied me no matter what I was doing—working with my students, going to a movie with David, or even taking care of Elizabeth. Although my family and good friends knew I'd miscarried two babies, I felt more sorrow than anyone other than David, and perhaps my doctor, realized.

I read what books I could find about miscarriage, resisted my doctor's gentle suggestion that perhaps I needed to go to a support group for a while, and felt depressed. I wrote down my thoughts on paper when I couldn't sleep at night and during the day when I was particularly sad. Writing was a relief because I was accomplishing something that blended my professional life—working with words—with my personal sorrow. I'd tuck my writings away in the back of a wicker basket on my desk and reread them now and then late at night. They were for no one else's eyes. As I sporadically wrote over a few months, I was healing and coming back to myself. Eventually, I wrote an essay, "The Stones of Children," where I confronted my emotions in a more public way, putting some sort of control on the uncontrollable experience of miscarriage. I had wrestled with my losses and had something to show for them.

After I wrote that essay, I decided to use my interests in writing and editing as a public response to my miscarriages. In my reading during the weeks and months after my second loss, I craved not just the medical or psychological discussions of miscarriage and interviews with mothers and fathers who'd lost children. I also craved emotional links: the voices of everyday people writing about and responding to their miscarriages. I longed for a chorus of voices telling stories from personal experience, but those voices weren't yet collected in a book.

I wanted to hear someone like Amy Desherlia talk about being a mother even though she had no living "child to see or touch." I wanted to hear someone like Deborah L. Cooper talk about working in her perennial garden where "all the fortitude, the stamina, and the effort associated with childbearing has been forced out through my fingertips into the soil." I wanted to hear someone like Altha Edgren talk about "moving past the pain to find a jagged peace in comforting another suffering sister." The voices of those women would have helped me work through my sorrow. I decided to use my essay as the starting point for a collection of writings—essays, journal excerpts, and poems—about miscarriage.

I told several friends about my idea and the more I talked about it, the more I realized that I wanted company doing this. The project would take a long time and perhaps be extremely sad, but it would fill a void in my life and, most importantly, fill a void in the reading material available to women. One morning I told my friend, Karen Fitton, about my idea and she said, "I've always wanted to work on a book. I'll help you." She had had a miscarriage before her two living children were born and she still thought about her miscarried child.

So began our collaboration. Together we would choose the pieces, I would do most of the editing, and Karen would do most of the administrative and computer work. Though legal dates for miscarriage vary, we defined miscarriage as a loss within the first twenty weeks of pregnancy. That is the date most used to separate miscarriage from stillbirth. We began gathering the writings by putting out calls for manuscripts through advertisements in magazines, notices in bereavement newsletters, fliers in women's clinics, and word of mouth. And the writings started coming to us in the mail.

As we read those essays, journal entries, and poems we heard the echoing heartache of not having a baby to hold and care for; the overwhelming grief that sometimes husbands couldn't quite understand; and the devastation of one day being pregnant and the next day having lost the child. We heard women talk about being treated awkwardly. We heard women talk about the sister-hood of sorrow—friends who had never mentioned they'd mis-carried told the circumstances of their losses with vividness and compassion. Through their writing, many women and some men confronted unfamiliar and complex feelings of loss and grief in a society that often doesn't acknowledge miscarriage as a death.

Some people wrote because we were putting a book together and it prompted them to put some sort of loving shape to their loss: a tribute to the miscarried child. Others had written pieces earlier and offered them to us as a way to help others who were suffering. Many told us that when their need was the greatest, they could not find a collection of voices like we were putting together and encouraged us in our work. And many thanked us for giving them an opportunity to write about their loss; the act of writing was important to their healing, even if we weren't able to include their pieces in the collection.

During those early months of working on the book, I had a difficult time deciding if I should try to become pregnant again. Being surrounded by the words of others who had lost children, having written an essay which put a sense of closure on my two miscarriages, and with the passing of time, I was coming out of my private, lonely grief. I wasn't crying much. I could talk to pregnant friends without feeling profoundly sad. I was becoming interested in my daily life. I was connecting with people with more enthusiasm. Perhaps another miscarriage would break my spirit further, unraveling the healing I'd managed so far. David, however, didn't want to give up hope for a child. We decided to try again. My doctor arranged for me to see a specialist so I could perhaps learn the cause of the miscarriages and receive advice on what, if anything, I could do to try to save a future pregnancy.

After six months of progesterone therapy, several uncertain months of rethinking whether I should continue trying, and then one series of fertility drug therapy, I became pregnant again. Within weeks I was bleeding. I was sure the baby had died, but an ultrasound showed the baby was alive. The specialist prescribed progesterone pills to take through my tenth week. A low level of the hormone progesterone after conception seemed to be a possible cause of the miscarried pregnancies. A week later I had more bleeding. Again, the baby was alive. I remained emotionally neutral as I felt it was only time until an ultrasound showed the baby without movement or heartbeat; soon I'd have a broken heart.

In June of 1993 when I was ten weeks pregnant, David, Elizabeth, and I boarded an airplane in Chicago and left the United States for a year in England. David and I were leading a study abroad program for our college. I had a bleeding episode several days before our departure. I was terrified I would miscarry on the plane and spent the travel time making plans for what I would do if that happened. But nothing happened and we arrived in Nottingham tired and relieved.

Soon, though, I had another bleeding episode. My midwives—every pregnant woman in England is cared for by a team of community midwives—put me on bedrest for the month of July. I read books about the British royal family and prepared myself to hear sad news about the pregnancy. I hesitated getting maternity clothes until I absolutely had to. I didn't want to make arrangements to borrow baby clothes or equipment. The baby was growing and I was gaining weight, but I didn't even want to talk to the midwives about delivery procedures because I could scarcely believe the baby would live to be born. My emotions were guarded. I put aside my work on the miscarriage book for nearly a year as I feared working so intently with words about miscarriage could jinx the pregnancy.

Despite numerous bleeding episodes during the first five months, this pregnancy story ends with a living baby—a child I could hardly allow myself to hope for, a daughter born a month prematurely and named Pearl after my grandmother. Though they could cite no scientific evidence proving bedrest can save a pregnancy, my midwives believed bedrest saved Pearl. I know a healthy baby won't be the ending for everyone, but I do know that many women, including contributors LaDawna Lawton and Dylan Ann Treall, did have successful pregnancies after their miscarriages. If I had had a third miscarriage, though, we wouldn't have tried again. My heart couldn't endure any more early deaths. I would have had to accept the reality that I would continue to be the mother of an only child.

In late June 1994, when David, Elizabeth, Pearl, and I returned to Iowa, I was ready to work on the book again. Karen and I had a stronger vision of what we wanted this collection to be and we gathered more writings, editing them when necessary to fit the shape of the book. We wanted a book that people could read from cover to cover or page through, stopping at the pieces that speak the most to their situation and emotions. These writings are not arranged by genre, but by threads that link one to another. Each can stand alone, yet they work together to talk about miscarriage. The words give the statistic "one in five" real names and real stories.

This is not a medical book or a guide on how to travel through the stages of grief. There are already good books of those sorts in public libraries, in bookstores, and on the resource shelves of hospitals and clinics. *Our Stories of Miscarriage* is a creative, literary approach to miscarriage: the voices of everyday people talking about and responding to their losses. Some writings, such as "My Second Baby" by Sarah Entenmann and "The Baby Rattle" by Dianne H. Kobberdahl, are factual narrative descriptions of the circumstances of pregnancy and miscarriage; others, such as "Ritual for a Miscarriage" by Kelly Winters and "Late Spring Poem" by Clare Rossini, are more creatively shaped reflections. Some contributors are experienced writers; some are new writers. Some write about recent miscarriages while others write about losses experienced years ago. All write from their grief and from their healing.

Karen and I have collaborated on this book for nearly four years. As we worked in the late hours after our children had gone to bed, we never gave up our dream for these words so lovingly given to us. We believe this collection of everyday voices will help comfort and give hope to those who are suffering miscarriages. It is a book we would have liked to have read, but could not find, in those lonesome, devastating weeks and months after our miscarriages. Finally, we hope that in the company of other mothers and fathers who have lost children, some readers will find the strength to write their own stories as a further part of their healing.

Decorah, Iowa
January 31, 1996

Our Stories of Miscarriage

BUDDED ON EARTH

Jean Streufert Patrick

I remember standing by the tulips at Kansas State University, shouldering a backpack stone-heavy with books.

Karen, another graduate student, rocked a stroller back and forth. Her black-haired baby drooled.

"So what's it like being a mom?" I expected something about sleepless nights and stinky diapers.

"You join the league of women." I must have looked confused. So she added, "You know. You join the ranks."

No, I didn't know. As far as I was concerned, I joined the ranks of women as a teenager when I bought a bra, sprouted armpit hair, and started my period.

I didn't think much more about Karen and her mysterious league of women until my husband and I moved to South Dakota. Church potlucks replaced graduate school parties, and we tried desperately to start a family. After months of praying, dreaming, and fervently reading every conception-related book in the Sioux Falls Public Library, I finally became pregnant.

That April, the peonies budded and my breasts bloomed. On a brilliant Saturday noon, I stood by the clothesline, hanging shining white sheets against a backdrop of freshly plowed fields.

What a glorious secret I held! So far, only my husband and my seven-month-pregnant best friend knew. Tomorrow I'd call my mom. She'd probably faint face-first onto her kitchen table. Her tomboy daughter was actually joining the ranks of women.

The scene that night was just as vivid. A bouquet of peonies sat on my kitchen table, their violet-red buds on the brink of blossom. Outside, the sheets hung still in the dusk. Before retrieving them, though, I ducked into the bathroom. There, on the cotton crotch of my underpants, were two spots of dried blood.

It couldn't be, I reasoned. Not after six months of praying, hoping, and pleading. But an hour later, the spotting resumed. Crimson. Then came the cramping, worse than any menstrual pain.

The next morning, in the sunny bathroom, I delivered our first child, a maroon mass, not even the size of a quarter. I wrapped our dream in a peach-colored tissue and laid it on the floor beside the toilet.

Under the hazy afternoon sun, my husband and I buried that part of ourselves. Using a spoon as a trowel, we dug a hole near a shelterbelt that overlooked the fields. As I knelt in the dirt, I remembered a weathered tombstone that I had seen in an old pioneer cemetery. The words marked an infant's grave: "Budded on earth to bloom in heaven."

The inscription should have been a comfort to me. What better place for a flower to bloom? But that bud—that precious bud—was my baby. I loved my baby. And I wanted to carry my baby for seven more months, or at least until she could bloom in my arms.

Every evening I lay on the living room floor. I cried. I bawled. I keened. From a phone four hundred miles away, my parents tried to say the right things. From across the room, my husband held strong, trusting in a future pregnancy.

Who could I talk to? Who could understand that a future pregnancy wouldn't replace my dead child? Who knew the blow of a prayer blessed with a yes, then crushed with a no?

Not Karen from Kansas. Not my seven-month-pregnant best friend with her seven-month pumpkin stomach. And certainly not all those fertile women from church with their flocks of children. The hurt was mine. The vast league of women couldn't possibly understand.

Two months later, in the heat of June, I conceived again. By July, I was queasy and green. But by September, I was ready to host the women's prayer league from church. Feeling domestic, I even made apple crisp. After all, I had once again joined the ranks of women.

I told them how thankful I was to have survived morning sickness, to have finally heard my baby's galloping heartbeat. Cautiously, I admitted that I had miscarried in spring. Their polite condolences I expected. But then came their own heartbreaking stories, given tenderly as gifts.

One woman delivered alone on her couch, her child just five months along. Another fell, losing her baby at six months. Still another suffered seven miscarriages before her first child was born, then three more before her second. Some bled for weeks. Others, like me, miscarried early.

Their stories carried bittersweet relief. I was not alone. Nor was I a newcomer to this league. As women, I realized, we aren't united by pregnancy and childbirth, but by our buds of hope and sorrow.

ALLEN

Amy Desherlia

Some people do not understand having a miscarriage means losing a baby, rather than losing a bunch of tissue. But I know differently. When I began having problems I went to the hospital to have an ultrasound. The nurse was not supposed to show me or tell me anything because I came through the emergency room, but when she was halfway done with her exam, she turned the screen so I could see the baby. I will never forget that night.

The sight of that little person kicking his legs and moving his hands made me realize someone real was actually inside of me. About a week later I went back for another ultrasound, but this time I could not see the baby. I was losing my amniotic fluid, so the baby was too hard to make out. I lost the baby two days later.

Before I miscarried, I was lying on the couch and told myself that if I lost the baby, I wanted to look at him. Half an hour later, I went to the bathroom and I passed him. I looked down and saw a little person about the size of my hand.

Ever since that night three months ago, I have felt empty inside and very lonely. I never knew how you were supposed to feel. This was my first time being pregnant. As the months go by, I have days where I feel too depressed to go on. I feel a lot of anger, but somehow I believe the baby is watching over me and giving me the strength to go on and to laugh again. Even though Allen was only with me three months, he will always be in my heart. I still consider myself a mother, even though I do not have a child to see or touch.

MY SECOND BABY

Sarah Entenmann

For a long time I thought that people who wept over miscarriages were self-indulgent and absurd. To treat a miscarried fetus as if it were a real child seemed ridiculous to me. Until 1986, when my turn came.

My daughter was two years old when my husband and I started trying to conceive another child. It didn't work. Month after month my body informed me that it did not work. But one sunny March morning (after eight months of trying) I triumphantly brought my pregnancy test tube into the kitchen to show my husband and daughter the good news. I felt excited and happy, willing to forget the wait.

Instantly I brought out my maternity clothes. I started sorting baby things and planning my maternity leave. Where would the baby sleep? How would my daughter react? Where would the money come from for two children? How much weight might I gain?

These questions drifted to the back of my mind as the weeks went by and nausea overtook me. Then a delicious drowsiness enveloped me. On Sunday, April 21, I lay on my daughter's bed napping; when I woke I was in a tender state of absolute bliss. I felt like a teenager in love.

The next day a small pinkish spot appeared. I had the kind of fear I'd known sometimes before—as my car skidded off the road or a phone call came late at night. Bad news was likely on the way and I felt helpless to prevent it.

But my doctor told me there was a fifty/fifty chance that all would be fine. I tried to hope for the best. My in-laws arrived for a visit and we joked about names for the next grandchild. I talked to my mother-in-law about whether I should have another cesarean. I rubbed my tummy.

On April 29, my daughter became very ill. We decided to take her to the emergency room, where they asked to do an x-ray. "I can't go in with her, I'm pregnant," I said. But when I went into the women's bathroom, I discovered bright red bleeding and knew that I would not be pregnant for long.

So that afternoon, after my daughter was medicated for pneumonia and put to bed, I returned—alone—to the hospital. Again I sat outside the emergency room. I watched a baby boy who'd been brought in for an ear infection. He had an older sister, and he was quite a lovely child. Oh, what a sweet little brother he was. His mother doted on him; his sister played with him. What a fine family, I thought.

The kind physician let me cry on the emergency room table. He did not feed me lines such as "You'll have another one" or "There must have been something wrong with it." Those lines would come later from other people. He put the stethoscope on my abdomen, but there was no heartbeat.

The baby, as if wounded, was slow to die. By April 29, I'd had a week of spotting, and I had to wait through another week of bright red bleeding. Tests showed that my body still contained "some of the products of pregnancy." My mind reeled, somehow thinking that the baby was in pain. I chided myself for my silliness, yet I felt like a horrible mother, unable to hold the child within me and unable to send it mercifully on its way.

On May 6, the fetus was expelled. Then I could "get on with my grief work," a hollow joke to someone who really hurts inside. Except for my daughter, nothing could fill my arms; my husband's lovemaking reminded me of the painful outcome of that February night of love. I thought of animals who bellow for babes that have died or been taken from them. They are not required to second-guess their pain.

I stared at pregnant women, whose ranks—it seemed—had swollen to the thousands. I monitored obsessively the progress of a friend whose due date was the same as mine. Shopping for groceries on a brilliant spring day, I turned into each aisle always seeing a woman in her ninth month just ahead of me.

I heard the stories of older women whose miscarriages had been dismissed with old wives' tales or saccharin promises of future happiness. They needed to use my loss as an opportunity, finally, to tell their own story.

The pain lessened, finally, when my son was born seventeen months later. I came to understand that there had been something wrong with my miscarried baby. My experience helped me reach out to other women and men whose babies were never born.

I no longer underestimate the bond between a mother and her baby, no matter how tiny, in her womb. And as I sit here writing about my miscarriage, I still feel it necessary—nine years later—to cry about the child I saw only as an egg sac on an ultrasound screen.

LETTER TO ROBIN

Deborah Vaughan

Robin
You were to have been the harbinger of our
    second spring.
Your smile was to have warmed our
    late winter's chill.
You were to have begun our
    cycle again.

But, you came too early, little Robin,
    your wings too short,
    your breast too tight,
    your eyes unopened.
Still, our ancestry etched in your
    cheek and chin and brow.

In the rainy, autumn twilight,
    you came too early, little Robin.

You were to have been.

LILY IN THE GARDEN: EXCERPTS FROM A JOURNAL

Deborah L. Cooper

June 27, 1991

Trying to buy a house on Friley Road, our dream neighborhood. I told Paul when we walked through the gate to the back that this was where I wanted to be buried; it could be my home forever. Huge, secluded backyard. Lots of garden space. Fruit trees, grape arbor, fifteen foot hedge surrounding the property.

Storm Street went up for sale today. I try not to look at the sign. It opens up our house, my garden, to lots of strangers.

July 8, 1991

Storm Street has not sold yet. The house has never looked better—freshly painted, clean, and crisp. The garden is beautiful. Thirty-eighth birthday closing in. Retired from United Parcel Service management for two months now. Lots of time to dig in the garden. I'll need it to transplant all my perennials if we move.

July 14, 1991

Happy birthday. Twentieth-year class reunion last weekend. Some people never change. Just older faces and bodies that now come with spouses and children. And lots of remember-when stories.

July 28, 1991

Catch-up: Ev's potty-trained. Today he got out of bed by himself. Did the big poop. Lots of praise. "No big deal, Mom," he said.

We'll be moving sometime in the next few weeks. Storm Street sold. Cannot believe the money we made on that house.

Strangers have approached me in the grocery store, on the street, to say they recognize me from seeing me working in the yard or walking the dog. They tell me they came to our open houses just to get a look inside. Their compliments on my decorating style were well-intentioned, I'm sure, but I feel so violated that they peeked into our bedrooms, our closets, the private rooms in my life. I am glad to be moving. That house will never mean the same to me.

I've been digging in the beds these last few days. Dividing and potting all my perennials. My babies that, three years ago, were so vulnerable to the cold, the rain, the drought, the rabbits. Now they have grown into beautifully lush plants that I cannot leave behind in the hands of someone who knows not a tulip from a dandelion. I've potted about one hundred plants so far. Major transplantation coming to Friley Road! Paul just rolls his eyes. Ev calls me the garden mother.

Speaking of babies...my body has started to send me messages from a quiet corner within; I can hear a far-off whisper that is barely there.

If my calculations are correct, we could be talking sore bottom, night feedings, and poopy diapers come next spring. What if I really am pregnant? What will another pregnancy do to my body at this age? How can I possibly keep up with Ev, settle into the new house, and work my garden? No way! Just thinking about the move to Friley makes my head hurt.

On the other hand...a baby. Nuzzling that soft baby fuzz. I still can smell those early morning hours with Baby Evan and my big milky breasts. I guess now is as good a time as any. Ev needs a sibling. We all would welcome a new baby into our family.

∗

August 4, 1991

I just know I'm pregnant. I'll go in for the test tomorrow to confirm. Nausea, so tired, legs ache, breasts hurt.

I told Ev. He says he doesn't care if it is "a boy or a sister." He'll be a great big brother. This is a nice secret to keep for a few days.

∗

August 5, 1991

Pregnancy confirmed. April 11 due date. My, oh my, what a wonderful day.

How to tell Dad-eo? Ev and I boxed up Billy Bobby Baby doll ("in diapers, pj's, and blanket," he instructed), enclosing a note that read, "Here we go again!" We delivered the package to the front desk at Paul's workplace. After the receptionist paged him to pick up the parcel, we hid around the corner. The box was marked "open immediately," so we watched as he pulled out Billy Bobby Baby and read the note. Ev broke from my arms and ran to his dad announcing, "We're having a baby!"

∗

August 12, 1991

Nausea, hot flashes, achy legs. Tired, tired, tired. Yes, Deb's pregnant again. I have a baby growing inside this old body. A first pregnancy at thirty-five was exhilarating, but now being closer to forty, I wonder.

I'm healthy and I'm going to have a baby. Ev's curious. Asks why I'm pregnant; where I keep the baby.

*

September 4, 1991

Not quite so nauseated these days. Maybe it means a girl this time. Feeling good enough to do some digging in the garden. Diggin' and daydreamin' about my little red-haired girl. Only seems right to give her the name of a flower—Iris, Rose, Lily. I like Lily. Lily in the garden.

*

September 19, 1991

Lost my baby last Monday evening. Morning sickness had abated previous Monday, so there was some question in my mind. Crampy around noon. Spotting by 4:00 in the afternoon. Taking a break from mowing, I felt that first trickle. Ev was napping; Paul was at work. I went inside to the bathroom to check and quietly closed the door. When I saw the bright red, I cried.

By 8:30 there was severe cramping (that horrible pain of impending delivery). Emergency room at 9:00 where the placenta passed onto the floor of the exam room. Operating room at 10:00. I'd never been to surgery or recovery, but was too sad to be afraid of the needles, the tubing, or the surgical instruments. Home by 12:34 in the morning. Had a mindless sleep. The first in months.

*

September 23, 1991

With renewed vigor, I've tackled the garden. Lots to do. I need to dig in the dirt!

September 25, 1991

Going to see the doctor in the morning. Checkup after the miscarriage. Makes me want to cry for Lily.

*

September 28, 1991

Finished stripping the cupboard for the dining room. Started building a picket fence out front along my flower bed. Have all the trimming and pruning done in the yard. Two truckloads hauled away tonight. Hostas in. Compost pile built and steaming away. Garden plot tilled and raked. Herb bed planted. Working on rest of perennial "transplants." I'm so tired and sad.

*

October 17, 1991

Lost my baby a month ago. Everyone says they're so sorry; it was meant to be; it's for the best; keep trying. But I don't know...I am sorry too, but I still wonder why. What horrible thing did I do?

I do know that Evan will be an only child. My window of opportunity seems to have closed and locked down tight. I am not willing to risk this ever again.

So lots of labor has gone into my garden these past thirty days. When a woman's body gears up for having a child, there are incredible stores of energy building within. The flower beds have become my decompression chamber to bleed off that energy, along with my grief and my pain. All the fortitude, the stamina, and the effort associated with childbearing has been forced out through my fingertips into the soil of my garden. If ever there were fertile hands, green thumbs. No one knows she's out there...Lily in the garden.

THE WAITING ROOM

Jon Masson

There's a reason hospitals call such space a waiting room.

There's nothing else to do but wait.

You look at the walls, glance at your watch, get irritated that the television doesn't work, and check your watch again. Only ten seconds have passed, but it seems like an hour.

I couldn't imagine what it was like for my wife, Patrice. I rubbed my eyes and then my face, stubble interrupting my fingers' path across my cheeks. How was she? When would I see her? She was nearby, but so far away as I sat alone in the visitors' waiting room at the hospital.

It was about ten o'clock in the morning on April 10, 1994. Who'd have figured that Sunday would wind up meaning so much? It surprised even me, once called "Mr. Spock" by a former co-worker. Stoics didn't let the world know what was going on inside. Mr. Spock didn't let them see him sweat.

This, however, wasn't a normal Sunday morning for us. A normal Sunday morning would have meant church or sleeping in.

Everything had happened so quickly.

Patrice was expecting our first child. She told me on a walk a couple of months before. Just about the time a jogger lumbered past us, Patrice said she was pregnant. I had matter-of-factly asked how her doctor's appointment went that day. The jogger and I were the first to know.

Patrice and I, like many others, married later in our lives. The knot was not tied the day after being handed a high school diploma. College, several years of work, and time spent out on our own came first. A few years together—alone—followed before we were ready for the next step: having a child.

I'm sure Patrice, at age thirty-three, felt more urgency than I did. I added eighteen to my thirty-four years to see if I still would be ambulatory when our son or daughter would be in prime athletic condition. The ticking clock, you see, didn't trouble me as much, except for the anxiety it could create for Patrice. At the moment, however, we weren't feeling any pressure, only elation.

The subsequent weeks were filled with future plans: how to arrange a room for the baby, how we'd manage our work schedules, how exciting it would be.

But Patrice preached caution and I followed suit. She said the first three months can be tricky for the mother and child, so we held off letting the world know the news. We told our parents, but asked that they not say anything either. How hard that had to be for my mom, who would have told only two parties—the Republicans and the Democrats. How difficult it was for us, particularly while on a vacation in March to our old home of Phoenix. A friend's wife found out she was pregnant and he immediately shouted from the rooftops that he was going to be a father.

We'd tell them our good news after the magical three-month mark.

It was about three months, as I sat outside surgery.

Nobody else was around—just me, sitting there, alternately thinking about Patrice and nothing at all. I guessed that during the week a nurse sat at the desk across the corridor to my left. I imagined others sitting there, as I was doing, waiting to hear how their wives or husbands or sons or daughters or grandparents or friends were doing down the hall.

"The operation was a success," the doctor would say, as relief crossed their faces.

Or tears would flow, when that other sentence, "I'm so sorry," began.

There was no hustle, no bustle in the room this Sunday morning. No cigars, either. Only a certain numbness.

Only a few minutes had passed since I found my seat, after wandering around the waiting area looking for a Sunday newspaper. Having no luck, I'd grabbed an out-of-date magazine. I considered my vending machine selection and whether I should eat it or save it for another two minutes. The butter crumb cake surprised me. Not bad for something wrapped in cellophane and inhabiting a vending machine capsule for perhaps weeks. The orange juice from concentrate was sour. Sweet crumb cake and sour orange juice.

I hoped Patrice was all right.

She had complained the day before that she wasn't feeling right. At four o'clock on Sunday morning, she woke me. She didn't know what to do. Her back ached. She had cramps. There was a bit of blood.

A couple weeks before, she experienced similar bleeding and told me she believed she'd had a miscarriage. She was certain. My spirits sank. Never having been through this before, and being uninformed about such subjects, I believed her. She was ecstatic after an examination showed she was fine, the baby was fine, everything was fine. Some women experience slight bleeding, the doctor said.

So I wasn't sure what to think, at four o'clock in the morning, but decided not to get alarmed. We'd have to wait and see what a doctor said.

Patrice couldn't wait. She wanted to phone the doctor. Unfortunately, her doctor wasn't on call. Should she call his partner who was on call? I didn't know. I was as indecisive as ever. Making snap decisions wasn't my strength. Now, before dawn, any chance of that was hopeless. I couldn't think straight. I had just woken up from a deep, wonderful sleep. How inadequate I felt. I didn't know what to say to my scared best friend.

She called, which helped calm her. She and the doctor decided the situation wasn't an emergency, but she should keep him updated. She called again a few hours later and said the pain was less and she would wait to see her regular doctor on Monday. Maybe it was nothing.

A regular appointment couldn't wait. Patrice still didn't feel well. She was nervous and wanted some answers. The doctor on call agreed to see her at nine o'clock Sunday morning.

I hoped for good news, but really didn't know what to think. I wanted her to be well. I wanted the baby to be well.

I tried to comfort Patrice, but I didn't know what was happening inside her. She could try to explain, but how could I truly understand? How can any man know what a woman is feeling during pregnancy? Or through its complications?

The doctor had me sit in the room while he examined Patrice. The only chair was in the corner behind where the doctor did his examination. I squirmed and looked toward the window. I felt like I was invading her privacy. The blood told me of the discomfort she felt.

Patrice and the doctor seemed to know what the news was.

The doctor had me look at the ultrasound screen. There was the fetus. Seventeen millimeters long. Sure, I'd seen plenty of pictures on television or in magazines, but I had never seen anything like it in person. That was our child.

I wish the first time I'd seen a fetus in person, the fetus had been alive.

I never had a strong opinion about when life begins until that day. That sure looked like a person on the ultrasound screen.

Eleven-thirty approached. My face felt grimy. Even one day's growth of beard made me feel unkempt. Lack of sleep the last two nights didn't help. I had joked before that I hoped our child would be a sound sleeper because I needed my eight hours. Now, that wouldn't be a concern. Suddenly, all the plans vanished, all the looking ahead ended. There was no baby to name.

The calls to friends and family wouldn't be to trumpet the good news. Instead, we would tell them that Patrice was all right after surgery. We would tell them she had been expecting a child, but had a miscarriage. My effort to report this news in a factual, unemotional manner would fail, my voice trembling and cracking as I stumbled to spit out the words.

Only the sounds of awkward silence would be heard on the other end of the phone.

And finally, "We're so sorry."

I stood as the doctor I'd met only that day reappeared. I listened politely, asked some questions, and watched him disappear. I could see Patrice in a few minutes, he had said. The anesthetic needed to wear off. She was all right. That was the main thing.

The doctor couldn't explain why these things happen, but said it's not unusual with the first pregnancy. It's the body's way of showing the mother that something wasn't right. The next time would be different, he said.

At the moment, that was small consolation.

We didn't want to hear statistics about other people. We weren't talking about other people. We were talking about us. Our baby. Our child, who'd grow up to be president or quarterback or literary prize winner. Or whatever he or she wanted to be.

We didn't want to hear about next time.

✳

I had never endured a day like that before, waiting so helplessly while someone I loved received emergency medical care. I had never endured a day like that before, when visions of being a father were erased before they were even fully formed.

I couldn't imagine what it was like for Patrice.

So I was at a loss for what to say or do as I sat on a four-wheeled stool next to Patrice. I smiled at Patrice, who smiled back. Her brown hair was rumpled, her arms hooked to tubes and monitors. She was the lone patient in a recovery room big enough for twenty or thirty gurneys like the one she was on.

My arms leaned on the gurney's side rail. I asked for details about how she was feeling and what had transpired in the last few hours. I attempted some humor, and she laughed. She was putting up a good front. I felt closer to her than I could remember. How alone she must have felt.

Patrice drifted off to sleep. I stared at the floor.

LATE SPRING POEM

Clare Rossini

I couldn't weather
Another March like this one,

The labor gone bad, the child arriving
Dead on a plush red carpet of blood,

So much lost

That my heart pounds frantically now
Each time I so much as
Walk up the stairs, turn in bed, cry:

The manufacture of tears
Requires energy, I know that now, I can manage
Just a few daily.

When I see the bridal wreath
Leafing out in the yard, that hazy, almost
Illusory green

I find it
Too much. I seem to have lost
All of my resistance to the beautiful.

So when my husband walks into the room
With tea, a single fresh rose on the tray—
Fresh bruise—

I break down completely.

Doesn't that ripe red know
How close to nothingness we all are?
Through the bandages of spring, earth will bleed again.

How perilously we are raised
By the ropes and pulleys of birdsong.

HOW MANY CHILDREN DO YOU HAVE?

Angela LaFisca

I have always wanted to be a mother. I am twenty-eight years old and my husband, Tony, is twenty-nine. We were childhood sweethearts and married in August of 1986.

Although I was not on birth control, it was not until late August of 1992 that I learned I was pregnant. I was elated. After my husband got used to the idea of being a father, he was happy, too. Tony's parents are friends of my parents, so we've been like one big family for all our lives. Our parents were constantly telling me they were ready for grandchildren.

When I was ten weeks along I started to spot. It was not very much at first but it still scared me. The following day I went for an ultrasound and that's when we learned I was carrying twins. I had wanted a baby for so long and had been disappointed so many times, but the minute I was told about the twins, I knew I would never deliver our babies. Things were too perfect to be really happening. By the time Tony and I got used to the idea that there were two babies, they were gone. Tony and I had a few problems at first with talking about our babies. I felt the need to bring them up daily, but he could not talk about them. At the time I was not very close to anyone else and he was the only person I could talk to. I went through a very hard time alone. It was heartbreaking for me that my doctor could not tell me the sex of our babies. The things I don't know about them still tear me up. I felt like such a failure.

In October of 1993, one year later, I was pregnant again. I was scared, but things were going well, I thought. My youngest sister and I were both pregnant and we had fun shopping for baby things together. One Sunday evening a friend asked me how I was doing. We chatted about my pregnancy and how I was going to hear the baby's heartbeat the next day. After I heard the heartbeat,

I would be able to relax a little. Miscarrying the twins had made me uneasy, though people, including my doctor, said it wouldn't happen again. That very night it started all over. I was reliving the worst nightmare of my life. Each time I walked into the hospital I was pregnant, and each time I walked out it was with empty arms. This miscarried child was a girl.

No one could tell me why the miscarriages were happening. My doctor said miscarriage was common and he would not test for a cause until I had lost more pregnancies. This time, those words were not enough. I did not want to get pregnant again until I had a medical answer. People seemed to think the answer was to try again right away, but I needed time to grieve for my children. The word failure can not come close to how I felt.

My husband and I built a new home and moved last November. For me, it was like starting over—a new home with no bad memories. I still have the things I gathered for our three babies and sometimes it helps me to pull them out and look at them. In the fall of last year I found a doctor who diagnosed my problem. I have an extremely low level of hormones and although I could get pregnant, I did not have enough hormones to form the placenta correctly for our babies to thrive. I am being treated and hope I'll be pregnant soon. I long to deliver a healthy baby.

I believe other people want to know what women who've miscarried are feeling, and truly want to help, but they can't know the empty pain unless it's from personal experience—an experience I hope never happens to them. Since Tony and I have been married, the hardest question for me to answer is, "How many children do you have?"

THE ULTRASOUND PICTURE

Karen Martin-Schramm

On my dresser is a fuzzy, black and white ultrasound picture of our eleven-week-old baby. It looks like a little person. Particularly striking is the large cord that connected the baby to me. I'm not sure where to file this picture. My miscarriage was a month ago, yet the picture, along with my pregnancy journal and a booklet entitled A *Doctor Discusses Pregnancy,* lies there, a daily reminder of my loss.

My husband, Jim, and I hadn't planned on having more children, so my discovery in April was a shock. I sobbed on the phone to Jim when I found out, feeling overwhelmed and fearful. Yet quickly I became excited and hopeful, and my imagination brought forward images of how the newborn would fit into our family. Given my miscarriage history—in between Joel and Joshua I had two losses, each at nine weeks—we had decided not to tell anyone until the first trimester was over. The secret only lasted for a few weeks, though, and soon we were telling the news to everyone. It was a grueling pregnancy, with a lot of nausea and fatigue, but I felt this was a hormonal sign that the pregnancy was really taking. I slept away the spring.

It took so long to become pregnant with Joshua that this "accident" seemed unbelievable at times. When I passed the tenuous nine–week mark, I felt more hopeful than ever. Soon, though, the bleeding started, and continued for three and a half weeks. Three times I had ultrasounds, each following days of very heavy blood loss. Much to our delight, the baby was fine, and was growing properly in spite of the clot of blood near the fetal sac. The baby was on the left side of my heart-shaped uterus, a troubling sign as my other miscarriages had also been on the left side. My two successful pregnancies had been on the right. Perhaps this was purely coincidental, or maybe there is an abnormality on the left side.

It's difficult to describe how hard those three and a half weeks were for Jim and me. Jim hesitated to bond with the baby as we could lose it any day. It was different for me, and probably for most women. Concerns and questions become all-consuming. "Do you still *feel* pregnant?" the doctor would ask. I analyzed every sensation in my body. (Is that just nausea or is it a cramp?) Going to the bathroom was frightening. (Would it be light red or dark red blood? Would I miscarry right now?) Having to examine every clotty substance that I passed, looking for signs of tissue, became ritual. Wondering if the next ultrasound would reveal a dead or living fetus was terrifying.

My last ultrasound was on a Friday morning. The technician was hopeful because the blood mass seemed smaller and the baby was growing so rapidly that the uterus was no longer heart-shaped. I was happier than I had been in a long time. Earlier that week the doctor, Jim, and I had discussed a date for my cesarean section—December 18 or 19 so the baby and I could be home for Christmas. The next day I felt queasy and exceptionally tired, not knowing whether this was good hormonal activity or a bad sign. By noon I was in bed, writhing in pain; I had never experienced such severe cramping. For two hours there was nothing I could do to get comfortable and I was vomiting because my body ached so much. I even wished "this thing out of me" because it felt as though my body was possessed by some demon. Then the pain vanished and I fell asleep. Upon waking, I went to the bathroom and passed a large round mass. I knew it was the baby: the embryonic sac looked exactly like the doctor had said it would look.

The miscarriage was at three-thirty in the afternoon on Saturday, June 11, 1994. I didn't want to leave the house. Jim had a work commitment, so around six-thirty he took the fetal sac to the hospital to the doctor on call. The doctor told Jim that he had never seen a more complete miscarriage and he showed him our perfectly formed son.

Jim came home and told me what the doctor had said. News of the sex made me wail for our baby boy. I thought back to the ultrasounds when I was trying to spot any clue as to his sex when he kicked his legs. When I had my earlier miscarriages, without having heard heartbeats or seen ultrasound pictures, it felt like the loss of what might have been. This time I lost a son. He was a baby whose heartbeat—like an answer to a prayer—was one I could see and hear when I thought it would be silent.

The loss of our child, even unborn, deeply touched people. Friends asked if we had chosen a name for our son and if we were going to have a funeral. We did neither. It was too much for us to bear or somehow too early in the baby's life. We were cradled in comfort by the kindness of friends and family. A friend of ours said it well: "To lose a child before birth is to lose a dream, a hope, and perhaps a part of one's self at the same time."

The miscarriage touched our boys in ways that amazed me. Joshua, at three, was too young to comprehend it all. I could tell, though, how afraid and uncertain he was about my tears and being in bed so much. Joel, at eight, had been my ambassador of hope. During the weeks of bleeding, he would be the one who would hug me and say, "It will be okay, Mom. The baby will be just fine." When I was pregnant with Joshua and bleeding heavily at nine weeks, four-year-old Joel sat down and drew a picture of our family for me. I was happy-faced, very pregnant, and inside my womb was a smiling baby. Like an icon, that picture of hope hung near my bed for my entire successful pregnancy.

When I miscarried this time, Joel followed Jim's directive and came into my bedroom, gave me a hug and said, "Sorry the baby died, Mom." He seemed to accept it and gave me the impression that he wouldn't give the baby any more thought. He did want to know when my grief would pass. "Will you still be sad tomorrow, Mom, and the next day, too?" A week later I heard him tell the woman cutting his hair that he would have had a sister "but she died." I decided I should tell Joel the sex of the baby. When I did, he looked stunned and sad. He could relate to losing a brother. Later he came up to me and said, "Mom, you're just going to have to plant another seed so I can get another baby brother."

A month has passed and I still feel a range of emotions. I've had spotting for several weeks, but like the ultrasound picture on my dresser, it's a daily remembrance I can handle. Telling the story of our loss to people has been good for me. Friends have listened and helped me process the mix of feelings. Some days I feel relieved we aren't having another child in six months as our lives are already so stretched. This, of course, elicits feelings of guilt. To add to my guilt I remember times I resented being pregnant—like when I sat in the doctor's office for another of Joshua's ear infections and thought with dread about going through it again with a third child. Other days I see a pregnant friend at the park or see a pink ribbon go up on a neighbor's tree and I am swallowed by grief.

Until two weeks after the miscarriage, I woke up each morning thinking I was still pregnant. I've had vivid nightmares that Joshua drowned in the city swimming pool while I was distracted watching Joel swim. I've read three novels in the past few weeks hoping for some escape, but, ironically, they have all been heavy and depressing, with some character who is miscarrying. Cleaning and organizing the house is my obsession, like a perverse nesting instinct. I am creating order and perfection now that I have my energy back. Questions still plague me. Should I have gone on bedrest even though no studies verify that it does any good? Why did I keep lifting Joshua after I had begun bleeding? Fluid depletion can affect the uterus and placenta; did I drink enough water?

Instead of treasuring Joel and Joshua like precious gems, I find myself being irritable and impatient many days. I've hired babysitters so I can have time alone to grieve and process my emotions, and have time by myself with my husband. The other night Jim told me that this third miscarriage was the hardest thing he's ever been through. I was surprised to hear that as many days I had wished he had been more supportive and understanding. During my pregnancy Jim couldn't offer me much comfort because he was nervous and afraid himself. At times it seemed like the uncertainty and the loss were happening only to me, but I know that's not true. We were both emotionally spent by the time it ended.

Later, I will be able to point to some wisdom I've gained by going through this miscarriage. But right now it feels like a gaping hole. In time the hole will close—well past Christmas when our son would have been home from the hospital. For now I am grateful for my faith, for the sense of God's nearness, and for my understanding of God as Mother: a mother who grieves with me while surrounding me in a loving embrace.

PUTTING TOGETHER MY BABY ALBUM: JOURNAL ENTRY

Robin Worgan

I go to the store to buy photo albums to put my dusty pictures in. I'm trying to be neater now, so this is necessary. It's $5.97 for big blue albums, $2.97 for baby picture albums. Why am I looking at these baby albums? I don't have a baby. My arm reaches out and I take hold of the small, white album with a curly-haired cherub riding a light blue rocking horse on the cover. I must have it. My hands caress the album, lifting each plastic picture cover—fifty of them. Each time I tenderly turn, I see a snapshot of what our baby would have looked like.

My hand moves down to my stomach, so flat, so skinny. Everyone is jealous of my thin body, my energy, my youthfulness.

"You're so young and you have your whole life ahead of you."

"I think it's much more difficult for older women to go through."

"You two have plenty of time. Just wait three months and try again."

"Oh, well, it happens to everybody. It just wasn't meant to be."

I would have been almost five months pregnant by now. As my hand, circling, rubs my stomach, I wonder what it would have felt like to have a voluptuous, purposeful body with a small life growing inside of me.

In my right arm I hold the baby album naturally, like a new mother holding her newborn for the first time. In my left hand I hold a three pack of soap. We are out of soap.

At home I pick out all the pictures of babies. They're not my babies, but babies I love: my brother's two children, my four girlfriends' children, my youngest four cousins, and my husband's cousin's daughter.

After organizing the angels in my album, I look through it again and again. Twenty blank pages are left waiting, like my blank stomach, like my empty heart.

RITUAL FOR A MISCARRIAGE

Kelly Winters

I wake breathing pain. *No, no, let it not be,* I whisper into the dark. Outside, the wind whispers back; the rain taps at the windows and recedes. *Yes.* I lie in bed, not daring to turn over. My pelvis is a chalice full of blood: if I move, it will spill. I am sweating and nauseated, chilled and trembling. The pain digs deeper and I breathe, flowing with it as I have been told that women in labor do, hoping it will pass. I follow my breath into sleep, but the pain wakes me from hope. I ride these tides of pain and sleeping and waking, listening to the wind, until the blood begins to fall, flowing out, a river I can't stop.

I am six weeks pregnant. I have kept the pregnancy a secret, feeling a quiet communion with the child, who was conceived in late winter and so, I imagine, will love this icy time as much as I do. Each morning I walk along the frozen shore of Lake Wingra, watching the geese and ducks who are returning home to the north. As the days go by, the ice on the lake breaks up, and puddles on the shore path are covered only by a thin sheet of ice, like panes of glass over bright pebbles. One day the red-winged blackbirds return, and I stare in wonder at an oak tree that appears to be fully leafed: each leaf is a bird, and all of them are singing. Can the child inside me feel the joy in my blood? In my mind I hold conversations with the child; I imagine walking along this same shore holding an infant in my arms or telling stories to a toddler I am leading by the hand.

Now all of these dreams are gone. The grass, green and new, seems like a liar to me, with its insistence on new life. How can I grieve? How can I mourn the death of someone who was never born? There is no body to bury, no funeral, no rite to ease the passage.

Before my bleeding stops, I save one of the cotton pads I have used to catch the blood, and use it to stuff a rag doll: the image of the child I will never have. I make the doll of soft peach-colored cotton, with hair of silk thread, embroidered eyes and mouth, and a heart-shaped bead over the heart. I sew it tiny clothes. Each stitch is an emblem of grief.

On a cool, misty day in early spring I get into my car, put the doll tenderly on my lap, and drive north, past black and white cows on hillsides and contoured fields full of last year's corn stubble, across the Wisconsin River and up to the Baraboo Hills. The trees are still bare but the hills are shrouded in a haze of green: the future of leaves.

I go to Devil's Lake, where high cliffs circle deep water. All around the lake are ancient earthworks, burial and ritual mounds shaped like birds and bears, built by the Native people who knew this was a holy place. Crows call from the tops of pines and turkey vultures ride the updrafts at the top of the cliffs.

I enter the woods and begin hiking up toward the top of the bluffs with the doll in my arms. The forest is full of the pale, vanishing flowers of early spring: bloodroot, liverwort, Dutchman's-breeches, soft as a baby's skin. I stroke the petals but have to look at my hand to be sure I am touching them. All of the ferns are still tightly coiled, waiting to unfurl.

I go to a hidden place, where there is a tiny cave of red stone. The cave is just big enough for one person: it is a natural womb, a place for passage, a house of dreams. I kneel, and name the lost child for the first and last time. I rock the doll, and tell the vanished child everything that I will miss. Then I bury the doll in the rich black earth. I sing my grief into the darkness of the cave. There is no echo: the earth drinks my words.

When I think I can't cry anymore I rise and walk to the cliffs, where the turkey vultures soar at the level of my eyes, not ten feet away. I sit on a square red stone and watch them fly. Their wings are wider than my outstretched arms and they are as silent as owls. I imagine I can hear the sound their wings make against the sky as they turn: a thin, high keening, like the sound of a crystal glass. Then I realize that I am the one making the sound: I am weeping again.

It begins to rain, softly, a secretive pattering against the leaves. Down below, the ancient burial mounds, shaped like birds about to soar over the lake, seem even greener. I wonder if the vultures I see are the same birds the mounds represent: scavengers who gather death and transform it into flight.

The rain falls harder and the birds drift away, but I stay on the cliffs, letting the rain mingle with the tears on my face. I stand and open my arms and sing my song of grief, in the company of spirits, moving with the strength of invisible birds.

GREY FLOWERS

Evelyn Fielding

fragile life
I held you in my palm
like sugar sand
or ashes

and Someone
swept you away
swept you under the
rug of Time
oh it's been years now

but I grieve still

THE BABY OF OUR MEMORIES

Kathy Law

Even though we had a son in December of 1983, my husband and I were having trouble conceiving another child. We waited until Jonathan was over a year old and started trying for a second child in 1985. Month after month, year after year, I wasn't pregnant. I had gained a lot of weight after Jonathan's birth. I had started dieting seriously in early 1991, and by summer had lost about eighty pounds. Dave and I hoped that would help, but the weight loss only made my periods irregular.

In the summer of 1991, I went on a business trip with a friend to Chicago. I told her about my troubling cycle and that I had not been feeling well. I had had many sinus infections and the doctor kept changing medications, trying to find a cure. My friend asked if I might be pregnant; I said we had long since given up hope. She talked me into trying a pregnancy test in the hotel. It was positive. Dave was out of town on a trip, so I was unable to reach him. I told him when I came home on Sunday night. We were excited, but also concerned because of my spotting and the sinus medications.

I scheduled an appointment with my doctor for the following day and he found nothing unusual. We couldn't determine when conception had taken place because I had been spotting off and on since May. He checked the sinus medications and didn't find any information indicating they would harm my baby.

The pregnancy was fine until the first week in August, when I started to spot heavily. I went to the clinic and a blood test confirmed my pregnancy. During the next few weeks, I continued to spot occasionally and also had cramping. My emotions ran from ecstatic to worried. I found myself feeling ambivalent about being pregnant because a part of me felt something was wrong. I was trying to protect myself from being hurt if I lost the baby.

On August 14, we set up a booth at the Iowa State Fair where we exhibit and sell the crafts we make. I found myself tiring easily and I was cramping. The next day, the first day of the fair, I started to feel worse and was spotting a bit. I left the booth and went to the camper we were staying in. Jonathan, Dave, and the friends who we shared our booth with stayed to take care of our exhibit. Dave told me he would be up at four o'clock that afternoon to check on me. Around three o'clock I had a severe cramp and felt a gush of fluid. I ran to the bathroom, sat on the toilet, and saw blood flowing steadily. I was scared and started crying. I thought of a story I had read that said if a woman passed anything while having a miscarriage, she should save it. I wanted to be at a hospital if that happened. I couldn't reach Dave at the booth, so I waited. He didn't come when he said he would, so I wrote him a note. I put a towel in a clean pair of shorts and went out to our pickup. I had trouble getting it started and I began screaming and crying. I was bleeding heavily.

I was ninety miles away from my own hospital, so I went to the only hospital in Des Moines I knew how to get to. Traffic was heavy and it took me about fifteen minutes to get to the emergency room. I told the medical personnel I was miscarrying. At first they didn't take me seriously because I had driven myself and seemed calm. Finally, after filling out numerous forms, I was examined by a young doctor who wasn't sure if I was miscarrying. He and the nurse left me alone in the room. I began to feel nauseated and faint. I couldn't reach the call button, so I screamed for someone to come.

An obstetrician came shortly before Dave and Jonathan arrived. He examined me, said I was miscarrying, and advised a D&C immediately. I asked Dave to call our families. After the D&C, I stayed the night in a hospital room. Dave stayed with me and our friends came for Jonathan. A nurse told me she had miscarried away from home, too, and if I needed someone to talk to, she would come. I was too much in shock to realize what had happened, so I didn't talk much with her. In the middle of the night, though, I began to comprehend that I had lost my baby.

The next morning I was released and went back to the camper. Dave had to get back to the booth, so I was alone. He hadn't called our families the night before because he was too upset. Dave had cried while I was in surgery and Jonathan had cried some, too. I thought my family would come when they finally heard the news, but they didn't. I needed to talk to people. I was devastated by the miscarriage and felt alone. Every night at the fair after Jonathan was asleep, Dave and I cried together until two or three o'clock.

I became depressed after four or five days. I was still cramping and had no energy. I felt terrible walking around the fair watching people having fun. I wanted to scream, "Don't you know what happened to me? There is nothing to be happy about!" My life seemed over. I even contemplated suicide, so I could be with my baby. The depression and mourning continued for months and I gained back some of the weight I'd lost.

Two years later, it is still difficult for me to talk about the miscarriage. I didn't have enough support from my family. They all said they didn't know what to say, so they didn't say anything. For a long time, I resented my family for not being there when we needed them. Dave and I decided not to try to have another child. I'm not sure I could survive the emotional and financial drain if I miscarried another time.

Dave and I planted a garden in our backyard in remembrance of our baby. When I tend my flowers, I think about my loss and feel at peace. I am doing something to honor the baby who lives in our memories.

GRIEF

Karen Chakoian

My assumption—and my experience—is that grief can be good. Of course, grief is painful. It's sad and hard and difficult. But grief can be useful and change a person's life for the better.

One assumption often made about grief is that it "happens" to people. Grief "happens" during a loss and is a collection of symptoms which must be endured. It is as though we are passive recipients of unwanted emotions, and there is an inevitable cycle of feelings and stages we must go through.

But it is a mistake to believe that we are passive ships being carried along by the currents of grief, to be thrown upon the rocks of pain and despair. Grief is an active process with a lot of decision-making involved. One of the main decisions each person must make is whether or not to be "swallowed up" by overwhelming feelings.

When I was four months pregnant, in September of 1992, my husband and I learned our baby had died. The nurse and doctor couldn't find a heartbeat during a routine prenatal exam. An ultrasound confirmed our fears. I'll never forget the devastating moment I knew the baby was dead. From there we had to decide what to do medically to remove the fetus and allow my body to return to a non-pregnant state.

A few weeks after our loss, I was at a turning point. I was worried that I would slip into a depression—it would be easy to do and I could feel myself sinking, out of control. But I decided that I didn't want to do that. I had some choice about my own reaction to the miscarriage. I decided to think about what to do to help myself—what steps I could take to process what happened and not succumb to the waves of sadness. I literally wrote out a plan. October would be my month of grief and I would accomplish as much of my plan as possible during that time. Not that my grief would be "done" or that I would never think about the baby after that, but it was a time-line for working on my grief and moving through it.

A grief plan is peculiar to each individual. There are no rules, no outlines, no guidelines, no givens. Other people will think some of the things a person will choose are crazy or inappropriate. That's all right.

Some of the decisions my husband and I made happened very quickly, by necessity, early on in our grieving. We had a chance to see the baby's body and we decided to do that. Next, we had to decide what to do with the body; we had the baby cremated and kept the ashes. We held a memorial service with a few close friends.

My grief plan was a blueprint for my healing. My first step was to write down everything that happened, so I could get it outside myself and quit rehearsing the story in my head. I planned to contact each of my brothers and my sister to talk with them about the miscarriage. Since there were significant medical complications adding to my trauma, I needed to sort through the medical side. I planned to read about miscarriage and to talk to knowledgeable people. In my plan, I anticipated difficult situations, like seeing people who didn't know our child had died. I knew that after a loss, people are more vulnerable to illness, eating problems, and insomnia, so part of my plan included practicing good health care basics like getting enough sleep, enough exercise, and proper nutrition. It was a good plan.

One point in my grieving process was particularly helpful to me: the time I spent sorting through what really happened. I think a part of all grief involves this—retelling the story, and sorting through the events that led up to the death or loss.

What's so pleasing is how much my plan paid off. Immediately I felt a sense of relief. I felt much stronger and in control, less vulnerable, and not so emotional. Over time, I became closer to all my family members. Our marriage became stronger.

By the time my plan was completed, I felt more sure of myself in all areas of my life.

This is not to say that my problems disappeared over night. It took time. For a while, I felt uncertain and even incompetent in my work and personal life. There was a period when I had a hard time making decisions and setting boundaries. My emotions were right at the surface sometimes—especially when there was an unexpected jolt. One woman at my exercise class, for instance, innocently asked how my summer was and I burst into tears. But I was recovering my sense of self.

Good grief happens best in community, with support. People wrote us notes, offering words of comfort and kindness, and sharing their own experiences of miscarriage and infant death. I understood why friends bring food after a death; besides giving people a meal they don't have to prepare, it is also warm and nurturing and represents the care of a whole community. A few people sent flowering plants that are still blooming, representing life and hope. And many people offered prayers, which gave me a whole new understanding of how prayer works. I had no interest in praying to God at all—I was too numb and too angry—but I knew that people were praying for me. I could not drown in my sorrow because I was being held above the waves by a whole community of people.

GIRL ON A GURNEY

Nancy Fitzgerald

She dreamt in the night
scarlet mist in her dreams
immersed in the mist
immersed in the red
as the shield she wore
cut through the placenta
cut through the placenta
and severed the cord
of the fetus.

Emesis basin,
crescent cradle which held,
crescent cradle which held,
curled and cold,
the perfect four inches
tiny toes and a penis,
curled and cold
it lay curled and cold
in the mist of her mind
for twenty-five years
in the mists of her mind
it was missed.

Girl on the gurney in grief
and alone
needed the women
needed the women
to say "No" to the shield
to circle the gurney,
circle the gurney

sing to the fetus,
lullaby to the fetus,
good-bye to the fetus.
Women to help her
get up and walk,
no longer a coffin,
away from the danger,
away from the mist
women to listen when she needed to talk
of the small scarlet scar on her heart.

APRIL 26, 1991: JOURNAL ENTRY

Jorie Miller

Friday. The first day of what would have been the eleventh week. We never made it that far. Late Tuesday, early Wednesday, the spotting that had begun Monday night turned to bleeding and cramping. The baby is gone. It is Friday, the third day of grieving. The wind shakes the old wooden windows. The birds chorus in a tree nearby. I have just asked Rose to turn up the heat. It is not a warm day, though the trees, bushes, everything that we expect is bursting with green life. Keith is fighting off the squirrels who will not leave the newly planted broccoli and pea seeds alone.

I love the flowers. Two pink roses in a vase from Sarah and Carol. The chrysanthemum plant from our neighbors Patty and Michelle. The exotic and lovely birds of paradise, fragrance of eucalyptus, too, from my sister Vicky. Dave and Carolina stop briefly to offer their sympathies. They bring condolence of food— French wine, cheeses, crackers, and preserves.

I have this urge to be by water. Rivers or streams that wash by me and under me and around and through me. To see and hear water move. It was a river that poured out of me. Gushes of water and blood. I did not cry when it was happening. Felt as if I had a job to do. The cramps made me whimper and wince. I kept my hands on my belly. Their warmth seemed to ease the tension.

And now, this sense of what—death? life? I remember the days after Rose's birth. I was euphoric. Then, like now, I felt myself the center of attention. Then, like now, I had hot flashes, was weepy. But this is about loss. The uterus I place my hand on is empty, not because a child has moved out into the world, but because a life has gone back to the universe.

But I am not lost. I am here in my life. In this world full of happy spring. I can't help but notice the tree flowers hang waxy from the stem. And my sadness is so pure.

MY JUNE CHILD

Sherri Rickabaugh

I don't know when bonding takes place for anyone else, but for me it happened the moment I was told I was pregnant. It was a feeling too powerful to confine to words—intense love, protectiveness, happiness, wonderment. I felt blessed and knew I could overcome any obstacle for the sake of my baby.

The joy was not to last, though. Within days of learning the good news, I began spotting. For the next week I lived in fear, pleading with God to allow me to have this child, and begging the child within my womb not to leave me. The doctor told me there was nothing I could do to prevent a miscarriage, but I stayed home in bed anyway. If I just stayed quiet and didn't move around much, perhaps the baby would live. I forced myself to eat nutritious food; I read inspirational books; I prayed.

The inevitable happened, but even then I resisted. If I could have pushed that perfect little eight-week-old embryo back inside me, I would have. As I baptized my baby, I memorized its every feature. It was too early to tell the sex of the child, but I sensed it was a boy.

Later, in the hospital emergency room after the D&C, I awoke to the sound of the most mournful sobbing I had ever heard. I listened as the doctor told my family that crying was a common reaction and then she patted me on the leg. I realized I was the source of that pitiful sound. I felt like a hollow shell—there was nothing left inside me.

That emptiness stayed with me a long time. The baby's father simply said, "It wasn't meant to be," and would never talk about it again. Other family members and friends told me that problems in pregnancy happen and I would have other children. They meant well but their words did not comfort me. I lost a baby, a being I helped create and loved. Miscarriage is not a death recognized in our society, so I learned to grieve privately.

My child would have been ten years old this June. I never forget a birthday and allow myself to daydream about what my boy would be like at every age. When I attend ball games, music concerts, school plays and other events for children, I wonder what my son would be involved in. Would he like the zoo, the circus, music, bugs, poetry? Every Christmas I think about how different my life would be if he were alive. Every Mother's Day I think, "If only my child had lived."

TWO CHILDREN

Natalie Magruder

I lost two children through miscarriage. My sadness and grief began on October 21, 1992.

My husband and I contemplated starting our family for three years, but because I was in nursing school we thought we should wait until I obtained my degree in May of 1994. But the waiting was unbearable. I was envious of every pregnant friend and stranger I saw, so in June of 1992 we decided not to wait any longer.

I found out I was pregnant in August. My husband and I excitedly told our friends and families. I was tired and running to the bathroom frequently those first eleven weeks, but I didn't have morning sickness. The pregnancy seemed perfect and I was eager for my first prenatal appointment. My oldest sister, who was pregnant with twins, told me it was ridiculous to be excited because the doctor wasn't going to tell me much that early in my pregnancy. I told her I just wanted the doctor to confirm my feeling that the pregnancy was going well.

At the appointment everything checked out fine, but the doctor wanted me to have an ultrasound to get an accurate due date. While the technician was doing the ultrasound, I looked at the screen and waited for her to say something. She moved the probe around and said nothing except, "Hmmm." She turned the machine off and said, "Sometimes this happens. The baby must have stopped growing. I can see the amniotic sac but not the baby." She pointed to the pictures on the wall which showed what the baby should look like at eleven weeks. Shocked by her words, I could not even turn my head to look. I felt as if my life was draining from my body. I was numb and tried to tell myself this was not happening. My husband tried to hold and comfort me, but I pushed him away. "How could I be pregnant but the baby not be there?" After what seemed like hours, we met our obstetrician in his office. He was sorry and told us I could have a D&C or wait until I miscarried on my own. I wanted it to be over so we set up an appointment for the next morning.

I was scared, hurt, and overwhelmed. Before the procedure I asked my doctor to do another ultrasound just so I could be sure that my baby was not living. This ultrasound showed the yolk sac, which wasn't detected the day before, but my baby was still not visible. Because of this, he wanted to wait a week before doing the D&C—just in case. We went home not knowing whether to grieve for our baby or to be hopeful. One week later an ultrasound confirmed the baby's death and, with my husband at my side, I went through the most traumatic and painful experience in my twenty-six years of life. I don't know which was worse—the physical or emotional pain.

Our doctor encouraged us to wait a month and try again. Since miscarriage is common, he felt the next time things would work out. After my miscarriage, I heard well-meaning clichés from friends and family: "You're young, so you can try again," "It was meant to be; there was probably something wrong with it," and "At least you were only eleven weeks along. Just think how horrible it would be if you were six or seven months." All of these statements made me feel worse. I tried to ignore them and kept a lot of feelings to myself. I attended a support group, Empty Arms, to help cope with my loss.

I had a hard time dealing with not being pregnant. It was unsettling that one day I was pregnant and the next day I was not. One day I could look at baby clothes and nursery furniture with hopes and dreams for my unborn child. The next day the clothes and furniture didn't pertain to me.

I wanted to become pregnant again, so we started trying to conceive. In December I had a blood test and nervously waited all day for the results. I was ecstatic when they told me the test was positive. I called my husband to tell him I was pregnant and we made plans to tell our families on Christmas. But our excitement ended when I started spotting the next day. I called my doctor. He told me not to worry and to come in for another blood test. So on Christmas Eve, my husband and I went to the hospital and I had blood drawn. Three hours later our doctor called to tell us the blood test indicated we were going to lose the baby.

My doctor advised waiting until the Monday after Christmas to have more blood drawn, but I never made it to the appointment. On Saturday I started bleeding. I was somewhat relieved that the miscarriage was happening on its own and hoped I would be spared having another D&C. The bleeding got so severe, though, that I needed to have the D&C to stop the hemorrhaging. Once again I was in despair and filled with sadness.

It has been five months since my last miscarriage. We decided not to try again until we had tests done to rule out possible causes. I have been seeing two specialists, one in my hometown and one at a medical school. They determined that my husband and I have an immunological problem and we have received treatment for this. Recently we have been told it is all right for us to attempt another pregnancy. I am scared, but not enough to keep me from the hope of fulfilling my dream of being the mother of a living child.

WHEN I LOST MY BABY

Lisa A. Harlan

After three years of marriage, my husband and I felt that we were ready for a baby. I read every article and book I could find regarding achieving pregnancy. After nine months of charting my basal body temperature, scheduling sex on my fertile days, and receiving five negative pregnancy tests, I bought my husband three pairs of boxer shorts. I was pregnant in two weeks. I was ecstatic; Mike was relieved.

Ten weeks later, on Friday, January 27, 1990, I felt small and occasional cramps. That afternoon I went to the doctor. After giving me a pelvic examination, he said the baby was only the size of an eight-week-old fetus. Since I was ten weeks along, I knew something was wrong, but I didn't understand the significance of the doctor's statement. I asked if the baby was perhaps just going to be small. He said that the baby had stopped growing two weeks ago. Even so, I just kept thinking, "The baby's growing. It's just smaller than most."

My cramps continued during my examination. Since there was no bleeding, the doctor tried to be optimistic. He made an appointment for me to come in Monday morning for an ultrasound to check and see if the baby was still alive. He said that if anything happened over the weekend to contact the doctor who was on call.

I started crying before I made it to my car and cried all the way home. I told my husband, and, as upset as he was, he tried to stay calm. Logically, he said we shouldn't worry yet because the cramping could stop. He said that if we lost the baby, we would try again. I know he was trying to help me, but I didn't want another baby. I wanted the baby inside of me. I had thought about this child's life: what schools he would attend, his daycare arrangements, who his friends could be. Mike was just as upset as

I was, but one of us had to stay in control. I couldn't; I went to bed and stayed there.

I was still in bed early the next morning when the pain started deep inside me—hard, sharp cramps, coming closer and stronger than menstrual cramps. Then I started bleeding. I called my sister. She had had three miscarriages, so she didn't try to soothe me optimistically. After I told her what the doctor had said the day before, she was very frank. She told me to stay in bed and said the baby probably had died at eight weeks.

When I phoned the doctor on call, he said not to worry. He also said to stay in bed and that perhaps the bleeding would stop. It seemed useless, but I went back to bed. The cramps got much worse. I called again. He said to keep lying down. The bleeding was too heavy for me to stay in bed, so I sat in our empty bathtub. The pain became excruciating, but I refused to take aspirin. I was reluctant to damage the baby. I knew the chance was slim, but if the baby lived I didn't want any medicine to reach him. The sane part of me knew that no tiny fetus could live through those strong contractions.

A short time later I called my mother and told her I was miscarrying the baby. I called my sister again for comfort and she said she was sorry. There was a surprise birthday party planned for her thirtieth birthday that night and all day I worried that I would miss it; it was easier for me to worry about superficial problems than to think about the death of my child.

After the third phone call to the doctor, he told me to meet him in the emergency room. My husband was watching football. I tried to be brave and acted like everything would be fine. Because it would seem serious, I didn't want him to come to the hospital. I drove myself. The emergency nurse was very gentle. The doctor confirmed my miscarriage and advised having a D&C in case some of the fetus remained. I was still hoping that maybe he had made a mistake. He insisted that wasn't the case. I called my husband and he came immediately.

The surgery seemed horrible. The medical personnel in the room talked about their personal lives while the doctor noisily vacuumed what was left of my child from my womb. I had never known grief before. No one I loved had died before.

The next day was a Super Bowl party at our house. I was dressed but pretty weak. I was exhausted, and sore, but I tried to act normal. Most of the people were Mike's friends, and I did not know them well. Mike had told them about my miscarriage before they came over. One woman felt embarrassed because she brought her two small children and asked if her children would remind me of my loss. I told her that I really didn't mind and that I loved children. I don't think my pregnancy loss had actually sunk in. I felt nothing.

I went to work on Tuesday and concentrated on feeling nothing. I accomplished this for two days, but on Thursday I started bleeding. I tried to ignore it but I couldn't. I had to ask my supervisor for a short leave. She told me to stay home until Monday. I stayed in bed for three days. My body needed the rest, but the inactivity was torture. I could do nothing but think about the baby. I was too depressed to read or to watch television. I stared at the ceiling for three days and nights and cried. My husband felt helpless and confused. He thought I was healing because I had acted fine for those few days after the surgery.

I cried daily. The crying sessions exhausted me and I finally grew weary of being tired. I limited my crying to an hour in the late afternoon before my husband came home from work. After four or five weeks I didn't need the release and I quit crying. I read as much material as I could find on miscarriage, which wasn't a lot. A co-worker who had two miscarriages gave me a book that helped. Slowly, I healed. My husband was supportive and we started trying to conceive again.

Four months later I became pregnant. Our daughter was born thirteen months after my miscarriage. I still think of my miscarried child and hope I never lose another child.

LAURA: A LITTLE GIRL IN A RED DRESS

Beth Lamsam

I remember the dream. We are at my grandfather's funeral. My husband and I are walking towards the grave site from our car. I am carrying our child—a little girl in a red dress, just old enough to walk. She slips from my arms and runs down the hillside towards the grave. As she squeezes through the fence her dress is caught on the wire. As I rush to catch her, she slips away leaving a few red threads caught on the wire and she falls into the hole.

I have awakened in tears from this dream many nights over the past two and a half years. The first time was the night I came home from the hospital after my first miscarriage.

While I was on sick leave after my first miscarriage, I read an article in a magazine; in it a doctor stated that women who lost pregnancies in the first trimester did not feel grief or loss. He said they did not consider the pregnancy real. What did he know? We were going to name the baby Laura if she was a girl.

The second time I miscarried, I had no complications. There was no hospitalization, no surgery, no sick leave—just a few visits to the doctor's office. I was pregnant. There was some bleeding, some menstrual-like cramps; then, I was no longer pregnant. It had silently passed. I had not told anyone that I was pregnant, so there was nobody to whom I could tell anything different.

But the dream came back every night for the following few weeks. And it brought the fears: What if we could never have children? Did I even want to become pregnant? Could I cope with trying to build up hope, knowing that it might be followed by loss and grief?

The third time I miscarried was during the ice storm in March of 1990. This one was much the same as the second one. I had no complications, just that sad, empty feeling.

I have read that first trimester miscarriages are nature's way of getting rid of a pregnancy in which something has gone wrong. As I put my son and daughter to bed tonight, I think of a little girl in a red dress and I wonder what went wrong and why.

BABY BORN WITH ANGEL WINGS

Jan Wagener

In a wisp of sheer net curtains
A baby born with angel wings
To enter life's muse too soon
And be stilled in a bassinet box
White billowy clouds surround
On a flight of wings forever
Anointed by my human hand
Child of mine wears a halo divine

MARKERS

Freda Curchack Marver

My husband and I had been trying to have a baby for two years when I dreamed that my sister, Trish, was pregnant. I lay in bed not moving. It was the first time I considered that she could have another child before I did.

Trish is younger than I am and I have always done things first. There were the growing up milestones: starting school, wearing makeup, beginning to date, getting a driver's license, graduating. Our parents made a big fuss over me on these occasions. By the time my sister got around to them, there wasn't as much hoopla. I had hoped Trish would get married before I did so she'd have the thrill of being first at something. It seemed possible since we both had serious boyfriends. I was surprised when Trish said she wanted me to go first so Mom and Dad could get the kinks worked out before it was her turn. The old pattern stuck. I got married before she did, and my first child was born before hers.

At the time of my dream, Trish wasn't ready to have more children. But the dream made me realize that even though my husband and I had been trying to conceive for a long time, Trish could have another baby before I did. The dream gently warned me of the shock and pain I might feel, giving me time to prepare for this possibility.

＊

Trish's first son was born at the same time my husband Jon and I began trying for our second child, before we knew we had an infertility problem. Trish lived out-of-town, and my daughter, Denise, and I flew down to help her care for the baby.

We had a wonderful time with newborn Gabe. I hadn't spent so much time with an infant since my daughter was born and felt a bit giddy thinking about becoming a mother again. Two-year-old Denise loved helping take care of her infant cousin—running into his room when he woke from a nap, carefully feeding him a bottle, and stroking him gently as he lay across her lap. She would be a terrific big sister.

I did not get pregnant the month we got back. Nor did I get pregnant the following month, the following, or the following. We consulted a doctor and learned that even though we had no problem having Denise, we were now infertile. The nightmare began: invasive treatments, multiple operations, and failed hopes again and again.

*

Three years after the dream, Trish was pregnant. I was elated for her and was optimistic about my ability to become a mother again. Recent test results were looking better. We had an insemination a week earlier and in a few days I would take a pregnancy test to see if it worked.

Those few days passed and then my parents called. It was the first time we had talked since we learned Trish was pregnant. They asked seven-year-old Denise if she was excited about becoming an older cousin again. Denise said, "Yep, but that's not all." There was silence on the line. My parents were cleverly indirect: "What else? What else are you going to be?" Denise wanted to drag this out as long as she could. She had been waiting to tell this news to people for a long time. Grinning and giggling, she twirled the phone cord in her hand. Jon and I made frantic hand signals for her to continue. Finally she spoke, "I'm not only going to be a cousin, I'm going to be a sister." My parents screamed. Denise laughed. Jon and I cried.

When I told Trish I was pregnant, she reacted as my parents had reacted: thrilled and relieved. They all were concerned about how I would respond to her pregnancy, since they knew Jon and

I had been trying to have another child. Now I would have a baby, too. All the pieces were falling into place.

I couldn't believe that my sister and I were pregnant at the same time. It would be exciting to go through our pregnancies together—monitoring weight gain, comparing when we first felt movement, talking about being hot and uncomfortable in the summer. Trish's due date and mine were only ten days apart. The cousins would be close in age.

Later that week, I had a miscarriage.

I didn't think much about Trish during that time. It was good that she lived out-of-town; I didn't want to be with her in the days and weeks after I lost the pregnancy. I was in shock, not really knowing how to feel. Strangely, the thrill of being pregnant stayed with me for a while. I was grief-stricken that I had lost the pregnancy, yet optimistic, because after five years of trying, we did conceive. There was hope.

I saw Trish several months later when we all traveled to my parents' house for a holiday gathering. I was nervous about how I would react when I saw her for the first time. I heard her arrive and got to the door just as she walked in, glowing with pregnancy. Under a maternity top, her abdomen had that wonderful bulge. She was very clearly with child. And I very clearly was not. My legs weakened and I wasn't sure I could continue to stand.

Before I saw Trish, my miscarriage seemed almost unreal. It was floaty, ephemeral, hard to pin down. I had no urge to cry, "My baby, my baby, my unborn child!" At the time I miscarried, I hadn't even felt physically pregnant. I hadn't gained any weight, my shape hadn't changed, and I certainly hadn't felt movement. When I had the miscarriage, it was more like a regular period than losing a baby. I even asked the doctor, "Was I really pregnant?" He assured me that I had been, as two tests had proven it. Yet if I hadn't been watching my cycles so closely because of the infertility treatment, I wouldn't even have known I was pregnant.

For me, the miscarriage was not the physical process of my body expelling a fetus. It was a series of images: asking a friend to pick Denise up from school because I was waiting to hear from the doctor; tracking Jon down at an out-of-town business meeting; hearing Jon say he was coming right home to be with me; sitting at the kitchen table at eight o'clock that night when the doctor finally called back to say that the amount of blood I'd lost was not unusual for the beginning of a pregnancy but that it should be monitored.

The images continued: spending days in bed as the bleeding intensified to a heavy flow; staying as still as possible to save the pregnancy; playing solitaire until the tips of my fingers were raw from handling the cards; having an ultrasound; hearing the doctor say there was no sign of pregnancy, then leaving the room so Jon and I could cry in privacy.

The images end with telling people about the miscarriage and their hushed tones: my not knowing what to say and their not knowing how to respond; telling seven-year-old Denise and seeing her confusion. "Is your stomach still going to get big and round?" she asked.

My miscarriage was abstract. I had lost part of a dream, some trust in my body. Oddly, I didn't feel I had lost a baby.

But Trish was a tangible reminder, a physical embodiment of what I had lost. I saw her and realized, "That's how I would have looked if I hadn't had a miscarriage."

I hugged her, but from the side. I tried to put my arm around her shoulder and kiss her cheek, but was not entirely successful. Feeling the firmness of her pregnancy against my side, I wanted to push myself away. As soon as I could, I excused myself and went to another room, careful not to let her see my tears.

The next few days weren't terrible. We didn't talk about my miscarriage and we didn't talk about Trish's pregnancy. Even Denise didn't say much, except for an occasional comment about how lucky Gabe was because he was going to have a brother or sister. I told her I understood how she felt and hoped she'd soon have a sibling, too.

One afternoon I went on an errand with my mother and by chance saw one of her friends whom I hadn't seen in years. She greeted me warmly and said, "Tell me, how is your pregnancy going?" I was so stunned I could not respond. My mother finally stepped in, "Trish is pregnant." The friend continued, "Oh, I thought you were pregnant, too. Wait, didn't you say both Freda and Trish were. . . ." She stopped. I stared at her just above her eyes so I didn't have to make contact. I didn't hear what happened next. I just wanted to get away. As I walked to the car, my mother tried to catch up with me, trying to explain as she apologized over and over. I was so hurt and angry I couldn't even listen.

I was surprised she had told anyone I was expecting a baby, given I was pregnant for such a short time. I suddenly felt exposed. Who else had she told? Did they know about the miscarriage? Who might we bump into next, and what would they know about me?

As we drove to the house, she was still apologizing. I knew she felt terrible. She had tried hard over the years to learn how my infertility treatments were going, passing on information she thought might be useful to me. Although sometimes her care and efforts to help me felt intrusive, I was grateful for her concern. That, however, didn't make up for what she had just put me through, albeit unintentionally. She wanted me to forgive her, to comfort her, to tell her it was okay. But I needed that comfort for myself and didn't have the energy to give it away.

My mother begged me to come in the house, but I didn't move. She wanted to make me feel better, but I needed to sit with my grief. She tried to change the subject. I did not want the subject changed. Then she offered advice. "Trish and I were talking. We thought it might be good if you quit work. Maybe that would help."

I was ready to explode. "What right do you two have to make a suggestion like that? Why is my quitting work going to help? My not getting pregnant is not because of stress. It's because of a physiological problem."

"I know, I know. But we thought you might feel better if you quit."

"I am feeling so low about myself because I can't have a baby. You're telling me to give up my career? Something that makes me feel productive when I'm feeling so unproductive in my personal life? Why would I want to do that?"

"It was just a thought," she said.

"Look, I know you have my best interests at heart, and I appreciate that. But why can't you ask me how I'm doing instead of telling me what to do?"

"Because when we ask you, you don't seem to want to talk about it. You push us away."

This dazed me, making things clearer and muddier at the same time. She was right. Infertility is so personal that I can't stand people prying. On the other hand, I want them to give me support. I want them to know what's going on, but I don't want to be the one to tell them. But if I don't, who will? Why am I the one who is suffering, yet responsible for taking charge? Why am I in desperate need of solace, yet supposed to tell everyone else what to do? Why do I feel absolutely certain that I'm not getting the support I need, yet don't know specifically what I want or how to get it?

But this was the wrong time to deal with these conflicts. I needed to take care of myself, not blame myself for my grief. My infertility and miscarriage were beyond my control. I could not do anything about the fact that my sister was pregnant and I was not. But I could say that my mother made a mistake by not telling her friend about my miscarriage. That was one thing I could point to, and, unfair or not, I wanted to blame someone for how horrible I felt.

I exercised what little control I had: I told my mother I needed to be alone. She squeezed my arm, opened the door, and got out. I sat for a long time in the hot car. I turned my head out the window, closed my eyes, and let the cool breeze dry my tear-streaked face. My tears left cold, dry, burning lines on my cheeks.

*

When Trish's son, Kyle, was born five months later, I flew there to help. Being with the baby was difficult, but I didn't want to let infertility control my life. I didn't want people saying, "She's so caught up in her own problems she can't even be around babies." I wanted to prove to myself that I was strong, and wanted others to see it, too. One day I would have a baby and Trish would come to help me out, I kept telling myself, so I wanted to be there for her.

By this time I had mastered my "door drop" coping technique. In a situation where I have to deal with babies, I imagine a heavy, metal door dropping like a guillotine. My anguish over the infertility lies on the left side of the door. The things I need to deal with are on the right. Whenever things get hard, I let the door clang down, and then I am able to go on.

One evening I was holding Kyle, not really thinking about what I was doing or whose baby he was. I had held him so much that week, while making dinner or running after Gabe or just watching television, that it felt natural to have a baby in my arms. Trish sat down next to me and asked me how the infertility treatments were going. I was grateful she asked and acknowledged that this was difficult for me. We began to talk and suddenly I felt physically ill. Kyle was too natural in my arms. I didn't know if I was embracing my nephew or fantasizing that he was mine. My heavy metal door dissolved. "Take Kyle. I can't hold him anymore," I said. I could no longer keep both realities in place.

Trish took Kyle. I talked honestly about my feelings about infertility and she listened. All week I had been there for her. Now, she was there for me.

A year later, Trish has two children and I still have one. Gabe and Kyle are seven and one, and Denise is nine. Jon and I continue trying to have a baby.

Usually Trish's children are simply my nephews and I love them as any aunt would. Yet sometimes, I cannot help but think of them as markers. Gabe marks the time we began trying to get pregnant again; each birthday he celebrates reminds me of how many years we have been infertile. Kyle marks the age of the child we never had. Sometimes when he hits a new milestone—rolling over, getting a tooth, or saying his first word—I think back to the bittersweet dream of cousins just ten days apart.

ELEGY IN SIX PARTS

Clare Rossini

(For Helen, miscarried at eighteen weeks)

1

So, little one, you chose not to be—

Or death chose you, that big wave
That rises out of nowhere to consume and deliver.

—Took you quick, caught in the rope
Through which my body shuttled air and blood
Toward your budding self.

I will say it again, without poetry:

You strangled in the umbilical cord,
An irony even the Greeks
Would have found too obvious.

2

The night we conceived you, our passion rose
Like the moon working its way
Toward an arcadia of clouds.
We waxed round, we shined whole for a moment,
Then fell back,

Hearing for the first time the wind
That was breaking like surf against the house. *Storm,*
I whispered. Then we both drifted off, not knowing

That deep inside my body, you had assumed
The bright harness of new life,
The weather of invention raging in your cells,

While outside, the coldest winter in years had begun:

The earth turning its face
Toward subzero temperatures, sizable winds, the oblivion
Of record snowfalls.

3

I haul myself onto the midwife's high cot,
Exasperated with my new weight.
I'm tired, I'm in the grip of nausea—
Let's just say that the charm of pregnancy

Had worn off. *I'm sure we'll hear something today,*
The midwife croons. I nod and close my eyes,
Feeling her push up my sweater, spread the gel,
Then move something metal over my belly.

We hear weird, inner-body static,
Pops and cracklings that suddenly clear
Into your heartbeat, a meter so skillful
And steady it makes sound itself a story.

The blue fluorescents buzzing, sifting down
The pale light of beatitude, I weep.
The midwife looks at me, alarmed, relieved
When I say *It's so beautiful*—those, your first iambs.

4

For a while, we were more than two. We added up
To an inherent third, the smidgen
That our kisses had trolled for.
We had got with child and life was good:

In every pot, a chicken; in every cloud, a God.
When we lay coldly, ash to ash,
Something of us would yet weigh earth down, yea,
Our protoplasm had found a new frame, and it fit fine.

Surely, child, you felt our happiness
Through the thin walls of my body.
Surely you knew what we knew for a while:

The glass filled to the top, the moon whole, the air
Ravished as the apple
Fell from the tree to the waiting hand.

5

Coming home from the hospital,
I find spring is up
And running full force,

The lilacs next to the bed
Smelling almost too sweet, as if
Trying to redress an imbalance.

Of which world am I?
That of a small box on the dresser,
With its plastic bag of ashes, light as silt?
Or that of these raw lavenders,
Trees scorched with blossoms, evening horizons
Done up in clear pastels?

I, forced to take up
The days, the weeks, the months,
That you refused to enter.

6

What are you now, dear?
Sand, dust in a shell, something underfoot,
Wave-lifted or falling? What now?

I sing a song of light disappearance,
Of a shadow earth never bore. I am glad
For all you never wept over,
The loneliness you won't feel,

The long empty nights on land. But dear,

Where are you now? What do you know?

We scattered you on the sea
On a mild June day, what little of you we had—
Substance of a small wind,
Heat used when the hand plays a grace note—

You were that light,
Dear, that light.

And how will the sea learn to hold you,
Small thing whom my hand held?
I will not forget your face,
No, I keep its memory near:
It had the sweet calm look of the late sleeper,

Sleeping your way
Through summer and spring, back to
The night of your birth, further back,

To the night of the kisses that woke you,
When the November wind
Hurled against the house.

I would keep you there, my daughter,
Still safe, nothing more

Than a hand lifted toward a breast,
A heart just beginning to beat faster.

GRACE

Betty Davids

My doctor came into the examining room and had a strange look on his face. "Yes, Betty, you're pregnant," he said. He then told me that this was problematic because my IUD was still in place. It could damage the baby. He wondered if I should terminate the pregnancy and indicated a large percentage of IUD pregnancies end in miscarriage, anyway.

I shook my head emphatically. "No," I said, "I could never do that." My husband and I already had three daughters and perhaps this baby would be a son. I asked him if there was anything I could do to improve my chances of carrying this baby to term and he said that I should just live my life as usual because what would happen, would happen no matter what I did.

I reached nearly five months of the pregnancy without any problems. One night, though, my back hurt more than usual and I couldn't sleep well. The next morning my back still hurt. In the early afternoon I started spotting and was scared. My husband, a trucker, was on the road so my sister took me to the hospital. For twenty-five miles I felt contractions and I had to lie down on the back seat of the car.

When we got to the emergency room, they gave me something to stop the contractions, but my water had broken. Soon the doctor told me that they were going to have to let the baby be born; grief and helplessness engulfed me. I promised to stay in bed and not move for the rest of the pregnancy, but my doctor told me that wasn't possible. By this time, my husband was there and we clung to each other.

One of the nurses stayed with me while the baby was being born. The doctor told me our baby was dead; the baby's lungs weren't developed enough for it even to have taken a breath. The nurse picked up the baby, wrapped it in a blanket, and held it like you would hold a living child. I'll never forget her tenderness when she showed me my baby, so perfect, lying still and quiet.

We told the doctor how important it was to know whether it had been a girl or a boy so that we could bury our child with a name and not just "Baby Davids." She was a girl.

We buried Grace Ann Davids on a balmy September afternoon in 1984 with her own headstone in our family plot. I was overwhelmed by the kindness of neighbors who I didn't know well and women of the community who came up to me to tell me their stories of babies lost and mourned. I had no idea there were so many.

Six months later I was pregnant again. This time a healthy boy was born, nearly a year after our little Grace had been due. Throughout the years, I've talked with my children about Grace, their sister who died. When John was four years old, he drew a picture of our family for his preschool teacher and he included a little bird in the picture. She asked him about it and he told her the bird was "Baby Grace, my sister."

No matter how many children you have either before or after a miscarriage, nothing makes up for having lost a baby. We would have given anything to have been able to save her.

EXCERPTS FROM LETTERS TO THE CHILD WITHIN

Jay Lake

June 4, 1995

To the Inner Child:

Today I learned of your existence. I thought for a week or two you might be joining us, but today we checked for sure. Your mom took one of those pregnancy tests and the line which said she was pregnant was big, wide, dark, and purple. I cried, a little; she stammered for a while. We have been waiting for you for eight months.

Back in February we thought you might have come. Susan was late, and we believed, for a while. I was bitterly disappointed when she had her period and you slipped away from us. Just recently, we discussed letting go of the idea of you. Not because we don't love you—we do and we did, long before you were born. But because we were afraid you weren't going to come to us.

Your mom's pretty old to be a mom. She had a baby once before—your brother Mark. That was years before I came along to be with her. We were afraid she would enter menopause—meaning she would never again be able to have a baby—before we made you. Hope was growing pretty thin when you showed up.

Funny thing. My birthday is June 6. Today, Sunday, June 4, we had my party at the China House restaurant in Lockhart, where my mom, Sarah, lives. (She is moving to Oregon soon, I think, so you won't know her in Lockhart. But what you'll know as Vicki's house is where she lives now.) The party was fun—we had Peking duck, one of my favorite dishes. The party was today, because I have to go to St. Paul for work and will be out of town on my actual birthday. Susan finally did the pregnancy test this morning, just by coincidence. You are my birthday present. The best one I ever had or ever will have. Strangely, you might be your mom's birthday present. You should be born late January or early February 1996, right around her birthday.

We already know a lot about you. Your name will either be Jade Ariadne Marshall Lake or Mercer Bryant MacInnis Lake. Subject to change, of course. When you read this, you will know.

We know what room you will live in, for a while. We know who your relatives are. We know who some of your friends are. We know we will all three move to Oregon some day to live near your Mamacita Sarah and my sister Mary Q. Maybe you'll have cousins by then. And we know everyone will love you very, very much.

I am writing to you for several reasons. My parents divorced when I was little, about three years old. I grew up knowing almost nothing about them as parents, their relationship to each other and to me. I know them both separately, but not together. I don't really know why they had me, or how they felt, or how I looked to them squirming and wet and red and shrunken like a little, damp, snot-covered prune that June day in the Naval hospital in Taiwan. I want you to know these things—to know you were loved from the moment Susan and I first dreamed of you. If something happens, somebody goes away unexpectedly, you can have these memories you would never otherwise see.

I want to remember me, too. I want to remember how it felt. When we looked at the little plastic stick, my eyes watered and Susan hopped up and down. I felt dizzy, dazed, and dumbfounded. One purple line had changed my life forever. Whether you become the first woman on Ganymede, or never come at all, Child Within, you are mine now and always. It takes love and hope and dreams to make a child. And from this moment on—when in your eyes I am a bright blur to your infant self, the trusted Daddy who never lets you down, the uncool geek who always embarrasses you, the old man on the porch—in my eyes you will always be my child. The dream Susan and I shared. Child Within, you will be golden. Someday you will read this and know, no matter what has happened over the years, that I love you.

I make no promises today. I will write to you when and how I can, Child Within, as the spirit moves me. That might be a few letters over the next nine months; it might be a regular journal for years to come. I carry a secret hope to be able to tell you the tale of your life, someday. Time and memories wash by like the sea. Maybe my writing will hold these moments fast so I can share them with you. We all go down to the sea some day, Inner Child, to the salty dark from which we came. Our finest moment is to raise another fish from the waters, help it cross the mud beach of evolution, and become a person better than ourselves. You are that person and I love you with all my heart and soul.

Sleep well in your padded cell. Susan will take good care of you.

Your Dad

*

June 5, 1995

To the Inner Child:

Hey, sprite. Today I went looking for something to get for you. Not to be unduly materialistic, but I wanted to buy you my first present ever. I bought you a little fuzzy yellow starfish and a plastic monkey for Susan. While I was shopping I saw a man in a wheelchair. I realized that everybody—big, little, man, woman, everybody—was somebody's baby once. I guess this is obvious, but everywhere I looked I could see someone else's Child Within. Everyone was loved once, just for being. Like I love you now. Child Within, you are waited for with longing.

I told my dad about you today. I tried calling yesterday, when I first knew about you, but there was no answer, so I called the office today. Dad was happy, but asked why I hadn't just sent an e-mail. I love him, but his perspective is sometimes different from mine. As mine will probably be from yours. Good night, Child Within.

Your Dad

*

June 6, 1995

To the Inner Child:

It's my birthday. I am thinking of the mass of cells that is you. Multiplying, dividing, an absolute mathematical genius at five weeks of gestation. Everybody who walks started out like you. Me, Susan, everybody. You. Jade/Mercer/love of my life.

Your Dad

*

June 7, 1995

Hello, My Sweet:

I didn't tell you, but Monday Perri Sigfrid said you would be a girl. I asked to borrow a highlighter from her. She hid a blue one and a pink one behind her back and made me choose randomly. I got the pink one. You are what you are and I love you.

I imagine you now, floating in the saline darkness. You are perhaps the size of my pinkie, maybe smaller, a mass of cells with a bump at one end and a hole in the middle. Such a small thing to become a person. My Little Fingertip, I am no longer alone in the world. I love your mother dearly, like life itself, but she and I are made of different people. Only in a child do you have a piece of yourself. Selfish, I know. Sometimes, I look at her love for your brother, Mark, and I feel a small, faint twinge of jealousy. Someone loves me like that, but I have no one to love with that elevator-falling, heart-and-soul feeling. Until now.

They say you will be born around Susan's birthday. It would be a happy coincidence if you came that day. She might not feel like that, but I do. Feel free to form your own opinions in future years. I know to some that might make their natal day feel diluted, less special, but to me it is fitting that the two people I love most in the world might share a day. No matter what your birthday, I will honor it always.

Who are you? Are you golden, like your mother? Flawed, like all of us? Special, like all of us? Your future is the mystery I cannot investigate, only experience. In the few short days since you wiggled into my life, I have come to appreciate and understand my parents more than ever before. That, too, is a gift you have granted me. Inner Child, I thank you from the bottom of my heart.

Remember me always, and I will remember you. Not yet born, and I know you. Old as I live, you will be new and unknown. Let us keep a faith between ourselves, to hold each other special and apart. I love you. Never forget.

Your Dad

✳

June 8, 1995

Hey, Rice Grain:

Susan looked it up and told me. You're the size of a rice grain right now. Tonight I am going to show these letters to her. Just wanted to say hello. I am tired. You must be, too, from all your growing. Keep pushing, little one. We love you.

Your Dad

*

June 10, 1995

Dear Child Within:

I am afraid. I am afraid for you and I am afraid of you. Your health and safety have become the most important issue in my life. I need you to be okay.

Susan started spotting today. This is probably normal, but it has ignited my paranoia. I am afraid you are slipping away from me on a small stream of blood.

I'm afraid of something else too. I'm afraid of Down's syndrome, of neural-tube defects. I'm afraid you won't be perfect and healthy. I don't believe I have the courage to raise a handicapped child. I don't believe I have the strength. Raising you will be hard enough if you are ordinary. If you are damaged, broken by nature's twists and our genes, I will love you as much as I do now, but I don't know how I will cope with you. And I don't want to be placed in that position.

Thursday night Susan wrote a message on the blackboard in our bathroom. It said, "Interactive Communications from the Womb: Hi, Dad (signed) jadmer@eworld.com." I laughed, a lot. Your mom is so great.

You don't have ears yet to hear my voice, but I am already talking to you. I tell your mom, "I love both of you." Sometimes I whisper into her navel, telling you things. Right now, my little Rice Grain, you are the child of my imagination. If I could will you safely into being, I would.

The world is a wonderful place just waiting for you to see it. I am filled with peace when I look at a sunset, or a rose. You will see these things, too. Do not let my fears infect your growing, Inner Child. Be strong as a little rice grain can be and remember someone loves you.

Your Dad

*

June 11, 1995

My Inner Child:

I am afraid we are losing you. This morning your mother had to go to St. David's Emergency Room because of excessive bleeding. They said her cervix was closed, so a miscarriage had not yet taken place, but one seems likely. She has bled much more today, although otherwise she seems healthy. Tomorrow we will go see the obstetrician to get the diagnosis confirmed and have more counseling.

I do not want to lose you. Your life with me has only just begun. I will always love you, even if you slip away. Please, if you can, stay close. My little Rice Grain, I am building up a heavy load of grief. I try to be positive, to help Susan and you and me. The fear and pain are very close to the surface and I shake when I think of how close I am to losing you.

The world is filled with rain and sun and flowers. You should live to run through them, not get flushed like a wad of tissue. My mother says if you must go now, it is probably for a good reason, that you weren't meant to live. But you are my first. Perhaps my only. I need you to stay; I need you to be healthy and happy and whole. The rain which falls, falls for you. The tears which fall, fall for you. I love you. Please live long enough to love me back. My heart hugs you, little Rice Grain. Stay safe.

Your Dad

*

June 12, 1995

Dearest Rice Grain:

Today I learned that you have left us. We went for an ultra-sound and they could find no trace of you. You are gone like yesterday's wind, blown into our lives and out again.

I know the medicine and genetics of this, at least vaguely. You were not meant or made for this world, or you would have survived. When the doctor told us there was no sign of a fetus, I knew you had bled away quietly. I shook. Missing you hurts.

Little one, you are as real to me as Susan is. You were only in my life for a week, but I will always remember you. First child of my heart, you will be special forever. I know that no part of you knew me, no part of you was big enough or complex enough to know or understand or, at the end, to hurt. But I know and understand, and now I hurt for all three of us.

I hope another child will come. We will give him or her one of the names we picked for you. This is not because we do not love you, but rather because we do. The next child will be a double child, always and forever. I will not hold you over the next child like a ghost or a threat. But I will always see you in that child.

Rest well, my little Rice Grain. It was wonderful to know and love you, even if only for a week. You are a small, growing dream which was never quite launched. Sleep the sleep of the beloved and I will dream the dream of the loving.

Always and forever,

Your Dad

THE BABY RATTLE

Dianne H. Kobberdahl

I started to think about having a baby in the fall of 1991. I'm not sure how the feelings started exactly, but they hit hard. I noticed babies everywhere and carefully read friends' and co-workers' newborn announcements. It was hard for me to believe I had earlier proclaimed that I would never have children because I didn't want to bring them into this less-than-perfect world.

Maybe I was just growing up. My husband, Steve, and I had been married for two years. We had had our time alone getting to know each other, we both had jobs, and we were in the process of buying our first home. All the pieces seemed to fit. The next step was to have children. After all, my doctor had said that he believed all good, caring people should have children because you never know if your child will be the one to make a difference in this world.

I went off the pill at the beginning of October. My initial reasoning was I thought the pill was causing some physical problems. I was also hoping to become pregnant soon. Steve and I had rarely talked about having children; we knew we wanted to have them but didn't know when. We agreed to take other precautions for at least another three months because we had heard that was best. We made no plans to try to conceive after that; we decided to see what happened.

One morning in early January I woke up and knew I was pregnant. I could feel conception taking place in my body. I didn't tell anyone, not even Steve. Two weeks later I did a home pregnancy test and it was positive. I was on an emotional high and wanted to savor the news by myself for a while. Thinking back, the reason I probably didn't tell Steve right away was because he wasn't ready for this news so soon. I decided to tell Steve on Valentine's Day and make it a memorable event.

I bought a baby rattle, wrapped it up, and gave it to Steve for his Valentine's Day present. I was excited; Steve was shocked. He didn't think it would happen quickly. I think Steve was happy to some extent, but also very nervous about the impending life change. We decided not to tell our families right away. Both of us are realistic; we knew miscarriage is common and didn't want to get everyone's hopes up just in case. I did tell my best friend that I was pregnant, but no one else knew the secret. It was the happiest time of my life.

I had my first prenatal appointment after eight weeks. The physical exam went fine except for the fact that the doctor didn't hear a heartbeat. He said not to worry, though, because the baby was just hiding. He asked me to come back in a week and if he still didn't hear a heartbeat, I'd have an ultrasound. I wasn't even very worried about it. One week later there was still no heartbeat to be heard, and there was no heartbeat to be seen on the ultrasound either.

I felt alone in that ultrasound room. It was me, the technician standing there, and a doctor I didn't even know telling me my ten-week-old baby was dead. Medically it may have been a fetus, but in my heart it was my baby. I've never cried so hard in my life. I cried all the way to my car and all the way home. I was almost hysterical, especially when I realized I had locked myself out of the house. I picked up a huge rock from our yard and threw it through the glass in the door so that I could reach inside to unlock it.

I'm not sure I felt any less alone when Steve came home. He was sad about the miscarriage, but he seemed a bit relieved because he wasn't certain he was ready for the responsibility of being a parent. I never saw him cry about the miscarriage, but perhaps he did. I cried for twelve hours straight that night. By the time I had a D&C the next day, I was too worn out to cry.

The next few months were horrible. Friends and family were sympathetic but not overly helpful. Looking back I realize there wasn't much they could have said or done that would have helped. I just needed to be miserable for a while. At the time I didn't know of another person who had had a miscarriage, even though everyone kept telling me how common it was. I got weary of hearing that. My miscarriage may have been insignificant to others, but it wasn't to me. A life had been growing inside of me and it had brought me happiness. It was a terrible loss for me, but not for anyone else.

My emotions were out of whack. I'd start crying long after people thought I should be over it. I was angry at the injustice of losing a wanted baby when unwanted, unloved babies are brought into this world too often. I was angry at Steve because he started putting all his energy into a new career. I worried obsessively that I would never be able to have children. I withdrew.

I finally decided to see a therapist for some counseling. He told me to keep grieving as long as I needed to, not as long as others thought I should. He encouraged me to write a letter and say good-bye to my baby. He let me cry and talk about my loss. Counseling helped me bring closure to the whole ordeal.

Four months later I was pregnant again and went to full term successfully. Now, a little over a year later, I have a three-month-old baby boy. While I will always wonder what my first child would have been like and feel I lost something precious, I know that had I not miscarried I would not have Jacob, my wonderful, beautiful son.

HER CHILDREN

Rebecca D. Anthony

In their eyes I see my reflection
or,
what was supposed to be
a piece of me
and I search their faces
for one of my own.

They prance about this woman's feet
and capture the embraces
once reserved for me.

I'm haunted by lunch pails,
skinned knees; midnights
of our children, never born.
My mirages scamper
amongst these blonde nymphs of hers,
imagined mine.
But mine of sacred moments
and forbidden doors,
born only in daydreams
and nightmares
were robbed of their dawn.
I see only my reflected image
in the eyes of hers, of his.

MIXED FEELINGS

Anne Walters

Not many people know what to do when a woman has a miscarriage. Most of the people I know see pregnancy as a sacred state of sorts, yet there is no protocol to follow when a pregnancy ends. People often treat women who've lost a child insensitively and without compassion. That happened to me when I miscarried away from home.

This insensitivity, unfortunately, shaped the way I initially reacted to my loss. I holed up. I didn't want to talk about my feelings of disappointment and sorrow. Closing up didn't do me any good at the time, except to give me solace from anyone else who might make careless comments. But by closing up, I didn't have anyone to talk to.

Not even my husband seemed to want to—or know how to— talk about the miscarriage. It was our loss as a couple and I felt really alone for a while. I think he didn't know what to say because he felt so helpless and, maybe, guilty because I had to endure the physical symptoms. I was miserable for the first week with nausea and cramping that sometimes left me doubled over. And it seemed like the bleeding would never stop. I bled for eleven days. When I passed what was never to be a child, it was like being in a room with an open casket. I was spooked and upset by it. I just wanted to be held.

My husband and I finally talked about the miscarriage two or three weeks later, when I was so frustrated with us not addressing it together that I started yelling at him. I accused him of not feeling anything. Of course, this forced him to talk about it, and it broke the silence that was making it worse for both of us. He was grieving, too, but in his own way. He had really wanted a baby.

The other side of having a miscarriage for me was a twinge of relief. Being pregnant scared me. I have no relationship with my biological mother and my stepmother has never given birth, so I had no mother to tell me if my fatigue and apprehension were normal. I depended on my nurse-midwife to tell me. I also read books that told me many women feel afraid during the first trimester.

I don't know if my fear of becoming a mother was normal or if I really didn't want to be a parent. Before I became pregnant, I thought becoming a parent was what I wanted. I have always said that I wanted to be a better parent than my parents were and being pregnant felt like an ultimatum: I had nine months to learn how to become a perfect parent.

And I know also that children change a marriage. I wondered if ours was strong enough to weather the changes. My husband and I come from such different backgrounds that perhaps we couldn't agree on how to parent our child. We talked about our ideas about parenting, but, as with marriage, it is not real until you do it. But now, I think the experience of losing the pregnancy strengthened us, giving us time to more thoroughly address the uncertain.

About a month after I miscarried, I started to feel better. I mentioned to friends that I had lost a pregnancy. Some encouraged me to talk about it; others said nothing, so I could say nothing further. Those who were kind listeners were the most helpful for me. Other women who had had miscarriages were sometimes helpful, sometimes callous. What helped the most, both with my feelings of loss and relief that I'd been freed from the ultimatum of becoming the perfect parent, were the sensitive people who did not tell me how to feel. They just listened compassionately.

Looking back now from my vantage point of having miscarried a child over a year ago, what I needed was a lot of support. The kind of sensitivity I craved but didn't receive enough of is what I try to give others when I can. This summer I was with a friend at a local baseball game. She was about three months pregnant and started bleeding as we sat on the bleachers. She lost control, and I knew instinctively to hold her and cry with her. I didn't want to be insensitive as people had been with me. Later, after she lost the baby, she told me how grateful she was that I had acknowledged her pain.

PIPIK

Susan J. Berkson

You win some, you lose some.

This one we lost. It was that one-in-five pregnancy that ends in miscarriage.

I'd carried it as carefully as I could: avoiding caffeine and heavy lifting, drinking milk, eating eggs and whole grain bread. We were growing used to the idea of a child. Having dreamed it (and worked at it and prayed for it) for so long, we'd envisioned how it would look, whose temperament it would have, what our lives would be like. We dreamed the homecoming, the naming ceremony, the first day of school.

We dreamed so much that when I got pregnant, bringing the dream closer, it hardly seemed real. We bought a book on pregnancy (soon to be referred to as The Book) and a CD-ROM, and began following week-by-week the growth of our little shrimp, soon to be named "Pipik" (Yiddish for bellybutton).

Our Pipik—we talked to it, cooed to it, dreamed of it, prayed for it. Pipik made his presence known ("Pipik" sounding like a him) by burning a hole in my belly each morning.

Until the morning the burning disappeared, the morning he was seven weeks old. *Happy Birthday Pipik,* I wrote in my diary. *You still look like a minuscule shrimp, but I love you nonetheless. I woke up without the now-familiar feeling of you burning a hole in my gut and I started to worry that you don't exist, that I am not pregnant, that mine was a false-positive pregnancy test, and all this hullabaloo is about nothing.*

So are you or aren't you? That is the question. Not only have I not had the feeling of heartburn, I've had a resurgence of energy and appetite, and not just for weird stuff like pickles—I want ice cream, cookies, chocolate, the food I always crave.

What does it mean? Steve says to enjoy these days because I'll have plenty of days when I feel bad. But, Pipik, I worry. I am only human. I suppose I should be taking yoga or working on some fulfilling project...instead I sit and daydream.

I can't see beyond my womb.

Your mama,

Susan

The next day, with big, fat flakes of snow falling, again I awoke with no heartburn. *Pipik, if you're not burning a hole in my belly, where are you?*

I was in the midst of changing doctors, so I chose to call the old, familiar doctor's office to report my symptoms.

Might I have had a false pregnancy test, I asked? The nurse snorted: "In the absence of a period or spotting and cramping, you're pregnant. Maybe the heartburn is gone for good. Count your lucky stars."

That night, spotting and cramping began. In a panic, I called the new doctor, who took a quick history and spoke to me in an informative, comforting way: "It could be normal," she said. "It could be the start of a miscarriage, in which case there is very little we can do."

I spent the weekend praying, worrying, cramping, and playing out various scenarios: 1) never was pregnant, had a false-positive pregnancy test, will sue old doctor; 2.a) ectopic pregnancy—fallopian tube will burst (meaning I'll never have a child), or 2.b) will undergo experimental procedure for transplanting fetus; 3) threatened abortion (which I found in The Book), where you almost miscarry but don't; 4) twins—one is okay, one is dying; 5) Pipik is okay, but it's a high-risk pregnancy and next six months must be spent in bed; or, 6) miscarried. Simply miscarried.

Which was confirmed by ultrasound on Monday morning. There you were on the screen, Pipik, exactly where you were supposed to be: in my uterus. We looked and looked and looked at the screen, "for a heartbeat," said the doctor. Over and over, the Disney song, *Dream Is A Wish Your Heart Makes*, played in my head.

You had no heartbeat.

Now I take aspirin, eat food with artificial sweeteners, and drink diet pop. I'd rather have you, Pipik. You were our dream, the wish our hearts made.

Asleep and awake.

We counted our lucky stars and you were it.

FRAGMENTS

Karen Fitton

The first time I heard the word *miscarriage,* I was walking up the stairs in our church. The news was whispered about a woman hemorrhaging in the bathroom. I was fifteen and had just come out of the basement Sunday school room. As my friends and I climbed the stairs to the sanctuary, we struggled to imagine what was occurring. Who was cleaning up the blood? How much was there? Did it hurt? Was she going to be okay? What exactly was a miscarriage? As the service proceeded and the pastor preached, we sat in the back pews, legs crossed, quietly writing notes.

There is a black and white picture hanging above my husband's desk at work. It shows two smiling people on a train somewhere in Colorado. My husband, Robert, his friend Rich, and I took a trip to Los Angeles via Denver on Amtrak in January 1984. I was thirty-four. Robert took the picture of Rich and me, developed the film, printed, and mounted it. Every time I view this picture, I think of the sad events which followed this happy trip.

As the trip ended and we drove home from the train station, I began to feel quite sick. I had been exposed to influenza two days earlier but hadn't given it another thought. The closer we got to home, the worse I felt. I went right to bed and remained there for over a week, with a severe headache, fever, sensitivity to light, and excruciating sinus congestion. My whole body seemed ready to die just to stop the pain.

We had planned to start trying to get pregnant as soon as we got back from our trip. It was this promise to ourselves that kept me going through my illness. A few weeks later I felt better and we went ahead with our plans. I became pregnant on the first try. Although I was tired in the eight weeks to come, I figured this was normal.

My miscarriage began with one sharp pain. The pain I had every month with cramping was severe but this was much more focused, like a giant pinch from a sharp instrument. I was packing some art supplies into a shipping container at the museum where I worked. I immediately sat down on the nearest chair. I felt a need to secure myself and counteract some part that gravity was playing. My senses told me that everything was not right. I feared I was not going to be pregnant with our first child. I hadn't even made it through my first hoop, a pregnancy test. (I had planned to do the test the next morning.) After calling Robert, I drove home to lie down. I was scared and confused inside, still hopeful outside. I probably just needed to rest more.

The next day, I talked to my doctor and we decided that I could remain at home. The worst was probably over and he asked me, if I could, to save any "products of conception." So far, we did not have any medical proof that I really was pregnant. I suddenly realized that the small, purple mass I had delivered at home that morning, examined, saved, and then flushed away had been some sort of fetal tissue. I started to cry as I wished I had something to show him. I was also angry at myself for rushing to try to become pregnant when my body was probably not fully healed.

In the following days, my life seemed to become uncoupled from the sense of time passing. I tried to keep looking normal. I checked the mirror often to see who was there. Inside, I felt bloated and ugly. I spent my time trudging from the couch to the bathroom and back again. One day, Robert took me out to breakfast to cheer me up. I sat in the hard, wooden booth at a downtown cafe and talked and laughed with our friends. But inside I screamed, "I just had a miscarriage and I'm bleeding right now in this booth and Robert and I are the only ones who know it." These friends would have been a great comfort to us, but I was afraid of my public reaction to their attention. An excess of emotions made me very fragile. Going out to breakfast took all the courage I had left.

*

Every summer since 1986, Robert, our children Reed and Jenna, and I travel to Virginia to visit Robert's parents. At least once during our visit, Robert and I sneak away to Williamsburg for the day. Our annual ritual includes a visit to the Muscarelle Art Museum at the College of William and Mary. Just going through the doors brings back the memory of our discovery of it while exploring the campus one hot, steamy July day. Our habit is to visit the second floor galleries first. We climb the stairs on a journey to see old friends. There they sit, in portrait poses, hands folded, waiting for us to appear. Colonel William Bolling. Mary Randolph Bolling. Mary with her delicate white cap tied under her chin, and her keen eyes. The colonel, looking steadfastly ahead, in his dress uniform. After paying our respects, we quickly look at the other paintings and decorative objects, and then hurry down the stairs to the main gallery and small adjacent galleries.

In the summer of 1994, there was an art quilt show in the main gallery and a West African artifact display in one of the adjacent galleries. Among the masks, I saw small effigies which had been carved for women who had lost children. They would carry these around to keep the dead child a living memory. This brought the woman good fortune for the next pregnancy. I had recently said good-bye to a friend as she went to England for a year, not knowing if she would miscarry again or carry a child to term. I had been thinking so much about her and our miscarriages, and I vowed to make an effigy for her, for myself. It was hard to leave that gallery. I wanted to stay a long time with those small effigies. They symbolized a life never to have been, and all of the pain of grieving had a place to reside. What a profound way to mourn. As Robert and I left the gallery, I felt as though I had been taught a new way to deal with loss.

*

My sister had a miscarriage in late 1993. It was her first pregnancy and very early, just like mine. She phoned to tell me that she was pregnant but had started spotting and now had to cope with the details of going on a business trip to London. I tried to imagine being away from home and hemorrhaging and not knowing if the baby had died. After she returned from London, a few tests revealed she was no longer pregnant. I tried to find the words to show I cared and I empathized. Perhaps the words written by a friend of hers say it all, "I can't really say I know how you feel. I only know how I felt."

This process of miscarriage is so solitary. It is comforting to have the unconditional, loving support of spouse, family, and friends, but in the end we are alone, in the bathroom, in the living room, at the grocery store, in a cafe eating breakfast, on a non-stop flight to London. We are silently struggling to pull in the pieces of who we were before this avalanche buried us.

FOR THE CHILD

Evelyn Fielding

silk ashes
rest lightly
in my palm
dream of you
a fragile thread
sewn by
trembling hands
quilted tears
o come softly
to my heart
I miss you

MY PRAYER

Jan Mathew

I pray that God will give you all the love that I cannot. I pray that my friends in heaven will surround you and let you know that you are not alone. I pray that, somehow, you know who I am and how much I wanted you in our family. I'll never give birth to you, hold you, or feed you. But I trust that, someday, I'll know who you are and who you could have been. I will never forget you. I pray that I meet you, little person, someday, in heaven.

✳

Nothing teaches you more about the miracle of life than a miscarriage. Once a life you have conceived is taken from you—even if the bond has spanned just several weeks—you are forever affected by the miracle of a healthy, developing life. You never take the gift of life for granted.

When my pregnancy ended, in October 1990, I was overcome by a sense of personal loss and, equally difficult, a loss of control over my body—and even over my life. I did nothing to cause my miscarriage and was powerless to prevent it. What I could control, however, was how my child, and my experience, would be shared and remembered.

I wrote a prayer as a eulogy to the child I lost. By writing this, I combatted one of the most difficult aspects of a miscarriage—the absence of a formal grieving or mourning process. A life—a soul—is lost, yet there are no public acknowledgments of this passing. There is no visitation, no obituary, no memorial service. My prayer somehow formalized my loss.

I talked a lot about my miscarriage. I was not obsessed, but I did share my story freely. When a friend or acquaintance I hadn't talked to for a while asked me when "number two was on the way," I wouldn't hesitate to reply, "I recently had a miscarriage."

For me, this was all related to the *formalizing* stage of my grief. I needed the public acknowledgment that my baby had died; I was in mourning, and it was fine for me to ask for support and comfort.

I also thought about my lost child in connection with religion. I turned to God, yet I admit, returning to Him was a gradual process. Although miscarriages are common, when it happens to you, you feel like one in a million and you tend to hold God, the creator of life, responsible. Did He single you out for some purpose? Did He want you to learn a lesson about something the hard way? Questions like these are normal parts of the grieving process, and for a while, can foster an ambivalent relationship with God. I had always believed that God played a role in everything that happened in my life, and that all events were part of His purpose for my life. It was natural for me to assign God a role in my miscarriage.

I eventually accepted the idea that miscarriages are perhaps a part of nature that God does not control and certainly does not wish upon us. He, in fact, mourns our loss and shares our grief. He does not cause our suffering, but offers to share its burden.

Time is a healer. Although it does not ease the pain of a loss, it does soften the edges. With time, almost in spite of your inclinations, the innate positive human spirit emerges. Gradually, often without consciously willing it, you find you have your concentration back, then your energy, and finally your desire to put your experience and your pain to work for the ultimate good.

Life is not entirely the same for me, but I accept the changes. I believe I have gained a renewed appreciation for life. I have learned that there are things I have absolutely no control over. My vocabulary is sprinkled with "hopefully" and "if"—especially when I talk about another baby.

I hold dearly to the notion that my child is in heaven and is with me in spirit. I live with the faith that someday I will see that little person, and that I will finally understand all that happened.

LONG ENOUGH TO HURT

Faye Ann Chappell

I never knew how emotionally painful a miscarriage was until I had one. I felt sad for women who had lost pregnancies, but didn't understand their emptiness and grief. I only understood the joy of a successful pregnancy where my plans and dreams came true.

From the start of my first pregnancy, I loved the little person growing inside of me and was anxious for us to meet. Would the baby be a boy or a girl? Would he or she have blue eyes like mine or green eyes like my husband's? I started a list of names and planned the nursery. I made a list of things we would need for the baby. I bought a teddy bear. I read books about pregnancy and childbirth, wanting to know as much as possible about the development of my child. I dreamed of what the baby and I would do together: how I'd show him or her to family and friends, how we'd splash and play in the swimming pool, how we'd go on walks.

When I became pregnant for the second time, again I started planning and dreaming. But about ten weeks into the pregnancy, I began spotting. My happiness turned into anxiety. This hadn't happened before. I called the clinic and my nurse told me that some pregnant women spot at this time. She said that I could be one of them or I could be losing my baby. On the eve of the third day of spotting, the spotting became reddish and I started cramping. My worst fear was coming true. I called my friends for prayer and then went to bed. Around one o'clock in the morning I woke up with severe cramping. I went into the bathroom and began losing a lot of blood. I dropped on my knees, pleading with God to let my child live. But I was losing the baby and nothing could stop the miscarriage. I went back to bed around three o'clock, only to wake at seven o'clock with more blood loss. I called the clinic and my nurse told me to come in immediately. The ultrasound only confirmed what I already knew. I was losing my baby. I went home to have my baby. One sharp pain and it was over.

It was hard for me to understand why I lost my baby. People told me it wasn't because of anything I did or didn't do. Miscarriage, they told me, is nature's way of getting rid of a child that isn't developing right. Hearing these words did not ease my pain.

We said good-bye to Christian Lee Chappell in a service. Close friends joined my husband, my daughter, and me in prayer and the reading of Psalm 121 from the Bible. My mother had chosen that psalm for her funeral service. Christian was laid to rest in a casket my husband made and his grave is marked by a cross my husband also made. We put flowers by the cross and still visit his grave. We want people to know about Christian and how much he is loved and missed.

It has been a year since we lost our baby. I have gone through a wealth of feelings—anger, pity, emptiness, loneliness and depression. The pain gets easier to bear, but I don't think it will ever go away completely. Sometimes it is still hard for me to see other mothers with their little babies. My arms ache to hold Christian.

Over time I have realized that my happiness and peace cannot depend on whether or not I have another child. Our five-year-old daughter, the living child of my first pregnancy, needs me. She can feel when I am hurting, and that hurts her. She needs me to be happy.

Another baby would not take Christian's place, but I would like to have one. We are still waiting.

JOHN CURTIS

Terry Schock

When you lose a baby the emotional pain does diminish in time, but a piece is always there. At certain times of the year—like the baby's due date or a holiday—it is sharper. You would not want the pain to vanish completely because it is a piece of you as a mother. You have lost your baby.

On June 3, 1988, I lost my first child. I had been pregnant a few weeks. "A blighted ovum," the doctor called it. My baby. My baby was real to only me. My husband was just getting used to my pregnancy and then the baby was gone. I named my baby John Curtis after both grandfathers—the only child to carry their names.

I remember how excited my husband and I were when I became pregnant. We had been married for twelve years and having a baby was a very conscious act for us. Our families and friends were amazed when we told them I was pregnant. It was very different when I told them I had a miscarriage. Telling them was one of the hardest things I have ever done in my life. I assured them I was all right; they did not know what to say.

I am amazed at the world's inept ways in dealing with mothers who have had a miscarriage. "Better that it happened now instead of later," they say. But to me, death is death. "You will have another one, try again," they say. But to me, one child cannot take another child's place.

After my miscarriage, I felt such overwhelming pain that at times I thought I would die from it. At times I wanted to die because I felt it was my fault the baby died. I thought God was punishing me for not being a good enough person. I am Catholic and my beliefs are very traditional. This blame was not a conscious one. If I could be a good enough person it would not happen again, I thought. But what if I slipped up? I hate not being able to control life; the people I love the most are at risk to out-side events. I abhor being vulnerable.

I know now that I was not being punished by God. The ironic thing about believing God was punishing me is that I have always believed God is loving and merciful with everyone but me.

I know it is not rational or logical but a small piece of me is still mad at God for my miscarriage. The one thing my anger did was give me strength to go on when all I wanted to do was crawl back in bed and stay there the rest of my life. Anger also made sure I would never forget my son.

When I first decided to write this I did not know if I could. Then I was scared; would all the feelings come and not leave? When I started to write it poured out so fast I could not write as fast as I could think. In this testament to John Curtis, I am one step further in my healing.

AN EARLY MISCARRIAGE: JOURNAL FRAGMENTS

Shelley Getten

Monday, May 22, 1995

Strange to be rereading my journals of death, when I am so full of life six weeks from my due date—this baby butting and kicking, ready to live—unlike the one before who slipped away too tiny to be felt or seen.

*

Thursday, August 25, 1994

First, a spot of blood, then more color the water; by phone the doctor tells me to lie in bed and elevate my feet. I try to keep the fear from rushing to my head, but cannot focus on anything else.

Brien hurries home; he takes our son to a neighbor and me to the lab where an ultrasound technician says she sees a sac—gives us hope. But the blood doesn't stop. Cramps begin to tear me apart. I am afraid to pee.

Next, at the obstetrics office a cheerful nurse sinks her needle deep in my arm for a vial of blood—our blood. The doctor says we should be hopeful, that I should rest.

Somehow I already know you are gone. I curl into pain, knowing I am empty, and in the afternoon it is confirmed.

*

Friday, August 26, 1994

Friends and family are near. I am amazed at how many have lost a child this way. They say, "It happens all the time" or "It wasn't meant to be." Still, I want a reason; I want to know what I did wrong.

A neighbor suggests it was too much vitamin C—and in fact, I was taking a lot. Perhaps it was the house-cleaning job I took or our lovemaking the night before—intense and wonderful.

*

Saturday, August 27, 1994

A florist brings daisies and baby's-breath from Brien's parents—finally, we are able to cry. Someone has acknowledged the life that is gone. Grief consumes us—we hold one another, make love in our mutual pain, want to make another child.

*

Monday, August 29, 1994

Once again, they take blood to be sure there's no chance of infection. I wait forty-five minutes as big-bellied women walk by—my mind goes wild with speculation.

Will I be able to have another child? What if there is really something wrong? The doctors don't do any tests until you lose two in a row.

I am in tears when my name is finally called. I ask the nurse for possible reasons—tell her about the vitamin C which, I read, irritates the uterine lining. She assures me there are no specific reasons—that "it happens all the time."

Then where are the other mothers and fathers—where can anyone go for support?

At what stage of gestation do the doctors refer their patients to grief counseling? A friend from work lost a fetus at twenty-eight weeks. Doctors sent her home to await contractions—the baby dead inside her.

*

Sunday, September 4, 1994

I don't know what I'm feeling. My little boy doesn't understand why I cry every day. Brien is baffled by my breakdown when I see a small boy with his younger sister and everything starts all over—tears and wondering whether we lost a boy or a girl and if I'll get pregnant again.

My mother frightens me more with her stories—an older brother I would have had was lost at three months, then she miscarried between each of her four living children. She says, "It happens all the time," and adds that I may have a genetically defective uterus like hers.

I dream of dead babies.

*

Wednesday, November 2, 1994

We are pregnant again! More cautious this time, not wanting our joy to overwhelm us. We will be on our guard to protect ourselves from being vulnerable again. I read books—learn to have confidence in my body and the forces of nature to help bring this baby to term! I'm imagining delivery—a warm squirming body in my arms, at my breast, alive.

THE SPIRIT OF THE CHILD

Dylan Ann Treall

My husband and I bonded with our baby before conception. We could sense the spirit of the child, waiting for us to be ready. We conceived the first time we didn't use birth control and jumped enthusiastically into the role of active, pregnant parents. We told everyone we knew, made plans for the perfect birth, began collecting used toys and clothing from friends, and signed up for prenatal yoga and childbirth classes. Having worked in childcare for the past nine years, I was excited to mother my own baby.

Many people shared their belief that Les and I would be wonderful parents. We agreed. We have a strong, open, affectionate, and honest relationship, and we know the importance of a healthy balance of nurture and structure. Our child's needs and emotions would be heard and accepted.

I had some nagging fears, however. What if I tried too hard to allow my child to express emotion? Would he or she clam up and not express any? What if my skills with children disappeared when I had my own? Would they end up thinking I nagged them too much? I was doing everything right in this pregnancy, but what if all the preparation didn't help and I ended up with a birth experience I didn't want? I was sensing intuitively that this was a boy, but what if I was wrong? Would I give a little girl the impression that I wanted a boy more? I had hopes for a Pisces baby—a birth at least a week later than my due date.

The pregnancy was going well until I had some slight spotting at eight weeks. It stopped and I quit exercising and stayed in bed more. I spotted a bit at nine and a half weeks and got scared. My midwife said to slow down and that we'd see what happened. The spotting stopped. Meanwhile, there was a part of me that knew I was going to miscarry. Maybe that's why I had so many nagging fears; it was easier to focus on whether or not the baby would be a Pisces than if he or she would be born. I scanned the plethora of books on pregnancy, looking for information about and symptoms of miscarriage. At eleven weeks I began having a small bit of brown discharge that went on for a few weeks. I stumbled across a sentence in a book about a second trimester miscarriage. It said, "scant brown discharge for several weeks." All my denials crumbled as I called my midwife through tears. I knew.

In the weeks following the D&C I tried not to think. I didn't want to think yet; I wanted to feel. Friends told the sad news so I didn't have to. I rolled up in a comforter on the bed, closed the blinds to shut out the late August sun, and cried. Les held me often. When he couldn't be there, I had friends over or talked to them on the phone. I wanted people to hear me cry. I was never alone more than two hours for a day and a half. Neighbors came by. Flowers were delivered. Many parents, whose children I cared for at the daycare where I worked, sent cards in the mail and told me of their experiences of miscarriage. I had no idea miscarriage happened so often. I didn't feel as alone. Many people understood the emotional pain of losing a baby.

Even though I had emotional support, I felt empty. It was as if an organ had been removed from my body and there was a hole there. I clutched at my abdomen, wanting it to be full, forgetting at times there was nothing there. When I cried, my empty womb was all I could think of. Sometimes it felt like I would never stop crying. At times, I didn't want to stop; I wanted to cry and be held forever. Then, the next instant, I would have a thought like, "I can drink a glass of wine now" or "I can do high impact aerobics again." I was startled by my bouts of joy. Until my friend Barbara said my feelings were normal, I felt guilty that I wasn't always sad. "It comes and goes in waves. Allow it," she said.

Les felt his grief differently, silently, and not as deeply as I did. At first I was mad and wanted him to cry. "Be sad! Don't you care?" I thought. He did care very much, though, and I had to leave him to his own grieving process. That was hard for me for a while. But he couldn't feel the physical loss; it was my body that had changed. His entire experience was different from mine.

After the first week, I cried less and less every day. After a few months I only cried at night and I would wake up Les so he would hold me, willingly, sleepily. Eventually, I began thinking about what I could learn from my miscarriage. I had already decided that this baby was coming back later. I was grieving time spent with my child, not a child lost forever. So I began my search for meaning with, "What did this child want to teach me?" I realized that I know how to get my needs met in a clear and direct way, and that there is a tremendous amount of love and support for me. I'm not alone. This was comforting, but there was more.

I thought about becoming pregnant again, understanding that each child born is a miracle. I looked back on my concerns in those first three months of pregnancy: have to know—boy or girl; have a trauma-free birth; give birth at least a week late; and relax with yoga. I was too nervous and was trying to control the uncontrollable. My fears of trying too hard were because I *was* trying too hard. I didn't let myself enjoy being pregnant. I thought, "Now I know what it's like to lose a baby, so when I get pregnant again, I don't need to know the gender, to have a trauma-free birth, to get the exact birthday, or to worry about making sure I'm relaxed. I just want a baby." I felt free with this knowledge. Worry and tension-free preparation was the best thing I could do for myself and the baby. I saw how I was creating my fear and I let it go. I thanked my child for the lesson. Because of my miscarriage, I would be a better mother.

I'm three months pregnant now and told everyone I knew right away. I jumped into the role of pregnant mother enthusiastically and I'm enjoying it. This time feels different, though. I'm more centered and balanced and I know the meaning of the word "relax." I can say honestly that I'm glad I had the opportunity to learn what I did.

TRIBE

Roseann Lloyd

i lost my baby
> it slipped away
quick as a fish
> dances
out of your hands
i lost my baby
> the other children say
we want
> *to see it   bury it*
it was so small
> i say but my hands
too want to dig
> they took
to writing
> but the slips kept
slipping away
the children persist   say *what*
> *did they do with it then?*
throw it
> *in the river?*
throw it away?
it was so small
> i say evasive
as a fish
> i see its shape
slipping across the
> doctors' tv screen
ghost sac: they called it
> couldn't tell me why
it went

away why

                    we can't bury it
        here

                    on the alluvial plain

downstream

                    another lost baby
                found
                by an anthropologist who
                      says the burial
                      6,000 years ago
                  was performed
                  with dignity
                  the baby
                      curled up
        like it's still inside
                  its mother

        the baby
            buried
            with ceremony even though
                it died at birth
        because
                of a spine
        that didn't close
                    the doctors
     can't tell me what part
   of my baby
            didn't open, close:
    fingers, spine, lungs, nose
how much how little

                there is
     to know i see

the baby's mother bending
over
the grave
my hands want
her hands' motion:
dig   wrap   hold

denied a grave
my hands
dig anyway
slip in the hole   sand
and peat and a young birch tree
it is so small i say
yet the leaves
already dance silver   in the wind
like fish in the river
ghosts of all the children
lost to us
in or out of graves
children dancing
along this river
the river that dances
down
the alluvial plain

OUR CHRISTMAS LOSS

Susan Geise

My husband and I get together with our families only several times a year since we live in different parts of the country. A few Christmases ago, my husband and I told my family the news of our second pregnancy. I was about seven weeks along. Since my first pregnancy was problem-free, I had little fear in letting my family know early on. They were thrilled and we talked about the new person who'd be part of our Christmas gathering next year.

That evening I began to spot. Not having spotted during my first pregnancy, I immediately became fearful. I called my midwife and she said spotting was not unusual and not a definite sign of loss. However, she said what would be would be and there was little I could do to change the outcome. The spotting continued and every time I went to the bathroom I was fearful. I wanted to feel secure that the pregnancy would go full term.

As the bleeding became heavier, my fears and my feeling of being out of control increased. After about six days of bleeding, I was certain I had lost the baby. I went to see my midwife, who ordered an ultrasound. My husband and I went to the ultrasound believing the baby had died. Much to our surprise, the technician showed us a live fetus and indicated that what she was seeing was very good: most fetuses who were attached to the womb in the manner ours was went full term. Our depression turned into joy. Once again we thought about a new child and felt a sense of relief.

I went to bed that night feeling excited, but as I lay there I felt labor pains. As the pains progressed, it seemed I couldn't handle what was about to happen. I went into the bathroom and became hysterical. It was as though someone was killing the baby and I could do nothing about it. As I sat on the commode and the child passed through me, a sense of helplessness came over me. Looking into the pool of blood, I couldn't allow the baby to leave me without seeing him or her. I put my hand into the bloody water and pulled out the small fetus. I took only a glimpse and handed the child to my husband. "We're supposed to save this," I said. Seeing the fetus assured me that there had been life in me and that I could grieve.

I returned to bed and felt empty. My husband became increasingly concerned about my continuing blood loss and called our midwife. If I had been alone that night, I would not have realized my hemorrhaging was endangering my life. I had an emergency D&C at four o'clock in the morning. In the hospital room afterwards, I felt taken care of and safe. I wanted to stay in the room for a long time, to heal a bit before I had to re-enter the world and face it as though nothing had happened, since I had nothing to show for my experience.

The doctor told me that people rarely see what I saw because usually a certain degree of deterioration occurs in the fetus before a spontaneous miscarriage. My baby had been alive that same day; I had seen a perfectly formed fetus. He expressed sympathy about my loss. As I left the hospital a nurse said, "Don't be surprised if this experience stays with you for the next six months or even a year." She thought I'd probably feel depressed. I was glad she told me, otherwise I would not have understood the complex feelings I was experiencing—and would experience—as I grieved. I returned home after eight hours in the hospital and tried to rest for the day. I needed to tell people about my loss and have it validated.

Several months later I received a letter from a friend with whom I had shared the story of my miscarriage. She expressed her sympathy and apologized for not writing sooner. When she received the letter about my loss, she was going through a tentative time. She was pregnant with her third child and having severe pain and bleeding. Her experience ended in miscarriage and she could not understand the meaning of it.

When I received her letter I was pregnant and scared because I was having some bleeding. I was soothed by her letter in regard to my loss, but also felt guilty that I was comforted by her loss. My third pregnancy went full term, but with three months of bleeding and other troubling physical symptoms. My healthy daughter was born; I again felt guilty when I thought of my friend.

I will never forget my miscarriage and will always feel a kinship with others who have lost a child. I have learned, though, that great pregnancies can produce great children, difficult pregnancies can produce great children, and suffering lost pregnancies does not always mean that a woman is unable to bring a baby to full term.

DYLAN, MY WIND SONG BOY:
MUSINGS AND JOURNAL EXCERPTS

Mary Lynn Hill

I am forty years old. Most of the forty-year-old women I know would be appalled at finding themselves pregnant. I was delighted, but also somewhat apprehensive of raising a child alone at my age.

I have two children, ages seventeen and fourteen. My husband and I were divorced in 1991, after seventeen years of marriage. I was devastated, but I picked up the pieces of my ego and began the journey of single life. I became involved with a man whom I care for very much. In April of 1992, I was diagnosed with breast cancer. In August of 1992, I discovered I was pregnant.

My feelings on discovering I was pregnant? Joy and a sense of awe at this life within me. Yet this was intermingled with fear and self-doubts. Could I raise a child alone at my age? I knew the answer to that question almost immediately, for from the very first day, I already felt the love and joy in knowing I was to be a mother again. I knew if I loved the child this much I could face whatever challenges motherhood threw my way.

So, I made the announcement to friends and family. There was shock and disbelief, but always support and love. I began to make plans, turning the den into a nursery, finding childcare, covering expenses. I made a list of names, mostly boys' names for I knew in my heart this child was a boy. I chose the name Dylan Connor.

One weekend at the end of October, I began to bleed—nothing heavy, but I called my obstetrician. He assured me it was probably nothing, but to stay in bed and remain quiet. My children were gone for the weekend. I was alone and very afraid. It was the longest weekend I ever endured. I was too numb to even call a friend. I could not bring myself to say the words out loud, "I think I am losing my baby."

The following Monday, I had an ultrasound and my fears

were confirmed. Somewhere over the course of the weekend, I lost my baby. The ultrasound technician was the one who broke the news. I was sent back to the waiting room to wait until the films were processed through. I sat there, alone and devastated. I tried desperately to hold back the tears, for I did not want virtual strangers to see my pain. As I struggled, the expectant couple next to me received good news; their ultrasound showed everything to be fine. I watched the relief and joy in their eyes and felt my pain move deeper inside me.

Over the next few days and weeks, I kept trying to sort through everything. "There must be a reason for my losing my baby. Why?" I had no answers, only a loneliness and emptiness.

Two months later, I found a lump in my other breast. Back to the doctors and again, another breast cancer and another mastectomy.

I still do not know why I became pregnant or why I lost Dylan. I do know that if the pregnancy had continued, the breast cancer would have flourished under the hormonal influence of the pregnancy. If I had been pregnant when I found the lump, I would have refused surgery or chemotherapy until after I had the baby. If I had refused treatment, my life would have been in jeopardy.

Did Dylan know all this? Did he end his life to save mine? I do not know. What I do know is that someday, I will meet my son and I will be able to hold him in my arms. Until then, I have been given a second chance, a chance to come to terms with all that life has thrown my way, a chance to help others who have had similar experiences.

Throughout all of this, I kept a journal about Dylan, My Wind Song Boy.

October 19, 1992

I have lost my baby. I miscarried over the weekend. I feel such an overwhelming sadness, such a sense of loss. I had already felt that baby in my arms, felt his arms around my neck, had already touched his hand and watched his smile. My arms ache to hold him and now I will not know that joy. I mourn his loss as I feel those dreams slip from my grasp.

Yet there is so much I have to be thankful for, so much support from my family and friends. Throughout it all, I have rediscovered and marveled at these people in my life. They have been there beside me, listening as I poured out my heart and soul, holding me as I cried and trembled in fear, and taking my hand as I forged my way through the fog. They have been my sun and moon, lighting my way as I traveled through these sad times.

*

October 27, 1992

I have learned to take one day at a time. Each day brings with it the unknown. The day may bring happiness or indeed it may bring pain. But no matter what, it brings life; it brings adventure; it brings with it a chance to feel, to experience, to touch, to learn, to grow and to discover.

Dylan, I was not given the opportunity to teach you all of that, but your spirit I will carry with me. You will be in my heart and dreams.

For the brief period of time that I carried you with me, I grew to love you and I mourn the fact that we could not share in this life together. But every time I hear the wind in the trees, I will think of you and short a time, our lives touched. You were a part of my wind, bringing with you life and hope.

"Wind Song," is an appropriate name for one whose life was so short, yet so powerful, for the winds come quickly and die quickly, leaving the echo of a song in the hearts of the trees.

The echo of your song is in my heart, Dylan, and will help guide me on my path in life.

THE ENGLISH REMEMBRANCE GARDEN

Deborah Edwards

They say every pregnancy is different and I think the same is true about miscarriages. The situations around my two miscarriages—the first in the United States and the second in England—were remarkably different.

February 1991—The United States

My first pregnancy ended in miscarriage at eleven weeks gestation. I remember first learning that we were pregnant on New Year's Day. Having wanted a child for a long time—I was thirty-five—and having just lost my mother six months earlier, I was excited to think about becoming a mother myself. I was confident that my pregnancy would go well, as my mother had borne four children without any problems.

Even when I started spotting at ten weeks I remained cautiously optimistic. I'd read that slight bleeding was sometimes normal and tried not to worry. After a day on bedrest, I was told by my clinic that there was little anyone could do to prevent a miscarriage at this stage and was assured that I could return to work. Just two days later it was obvious that I was in the process of losing my pregnancy.

What I remember of that early stage was intense pain, more painful than any period I'd ever had, and increasingly heavy bleeding. In touch with the on-call nurses at my local hospital, I was advised to remain at home until the bleeding was quite severe, enough to "saturate a pad an hour." Fortunately, my husband was home that evening and we waited it out together. We made the trip to our local emergency room at ten-thirty that night, where we waited at least an hour to see a doctor. Left alone in a small cubicle, bleeding helplessly, the only recourse I had was to hold an old-fashioned, non-adhesive pad between my legs as staff wandered in and out of the room. How humiliated I felt. Patient dignity wasn't a priority in that busy place. Finally, a kind young female medical student confirmed that I'd miscarried—and that I'd have to have a D&C in the morning.

To save hospital costs, I was never admitted. Instead, my husband and I spent the night in the extremely crowded outpatient ward of that prestigious, highly marketed hospital with a grand piano in the lobby. Nick slept on the floor, as there wasn't even a chair available. It would be difficult to say if the emotional or physical pain that night was greater. Emotionally, I was hit hard as the healing wounds of losing my mother were suddenly reopened. Why did she die so young and why couldn't she be there to comfort me? Physically, I felt waves of contractions trying to expel the damaged embryo. I needed a lot of sedation and could hardly wait for the next dose of painkillers. It didn't help that my nurse thought I was exaggerating the pain. "It's only a miscarriage," she said. I felt too exhausted and vulnerable to protest.

I had surgery at seven o'clock in the morning when my doctor arrived, and was home by ten o'clock that morning. I don't remember follow-up guidance except instructions to see my doctor in a week or maybe two. They said that they were sorry that this happened, but miscarriage is very common, good-bye. We were left to our own devices to cope with the loss.

Yet besides the emotional stress of losing my baby so soon after losing my mother, I initially handled this miscarriage quite well. My husband was supportive and my co-workers (I was working in a Bureau of Maternal and Child Health as a dietician) were knowledgeable and sympathetic. One colleague had recently lost twins at five months gestation. Compared to her, I felt fortunate. In addition, I was comforted by the fact that I had gotten pregnant so quickly and that, statistically, my chances of a repeated miscarriage were quite small.

If only it had been that easy. Month after month I didn't get pregnant and I began to worry. Now thirty-six and aware of my decreasing fertility, I finally discussed my fears with my family doctor, who referred me to an infertility specialist. It was not without cause, as my husband and I were told that we were relatively infertile, with only a thirty percent chance of conceiving in any five year period. A year after the initial event, the full ramification of my miscarriage suddenly became apparent. I might have lost my only chance to have a child.

Fortunately, within only four months of our diagnosis of infertility (a time that seemed like eternity) we became pregnant again. I will always consider this pregnancy the miracle of my lifetime. Actually, we rejoiced cautiously at first, wary of another miscarriage. But as time wore on we became more confident and I felt like the happiest woman alive. Near the end of my pregnancy, however, I began to show signs of hypertension of pregnancy. A few weeks later, my daughter was born after I had a harrowing and life-threatening experience of severe pre-eclampsia. Five weeks premature, but with the lung function of a considerably smaller infant, she spent two weeks in neonatal intensive care. My emotions were everywhere as I thanked God I was still alive but worried about my irreplaceable baby.

As the doctors predicted, my daughter did well and we brought her home in mid-December. Still a bit unnerved by the experience of pre-eclampsia and of having a premature baby, we threw ourselves into being new parents. I was thrilled to finally hold a baby in my arms. Nothing else mattered.

Our decision to try for another child was not an easy one. At my six week checkup, my obstetrician advised against it, saying that I would be putting myself at risk with another pregnancy. My family physician agreed. We were discouraged, but realized how fortunate we were to have one child. For six months, I put the issue out of my mind. But gradually the maternal instinct returned and we sought a second opinion from a high risk specialist at another institution. His report was more optimistic, but not totally convincing. A year later, another specialist scoffed at my fears and basically told me that my long-term chances of another healthy baby were excellent (although he/she might be born prematurely) and that my own risks of dying were exceedingly small.

*

July 1994—England

We moved to Nottingham, England for a year and the issue remained unsettled. How could I risk my life at all to have another child, when my daughter was so young? And yet, if the risk was small, why shouldn't I take it to give her a sibling? I sought yet another opinion at one of the best medical centers in England, just ten minutes from my home. My consultant assured me that my chances of having a healthy baby were excellent—if I could become pregnant again, of course. Finally, after two years of deliberation and emotional turmoil, we decided to try again.

This time it took only two months to conceive. Given our infertility diagnosis, and the enormity of our decision, we were elated and I was certain that it was meant to be.

*

November 1994—England

Our hopes were dashed at six weeks gestation. This time I knew what was happening and I was upset, but not afraid. My general practitioner referred me to a high-risk pregnancy clinic at Queen's Medical Centre in Nottingham. My care here, under the National Health Service of Great Britain, was phenomenal and, in some respects, a world apart from my care in the United States.

At the high-risk pregnancy clinic, I had an ultrasound to assess the status of my six-week-old pregnancy. The ultrasound revealed a three- to four-week-old embryo. The staff suggested that perhaps we'd miscalculated. Sadly, we knew that our dates were correct. I was then sent home with instructions to rest and to call if the bleeding intensified. Even though the ultrasound result was not good news, we appreciated being informed quickly.

Two days later the miscarriage intensified. I called the nurse practitioner and will never forget her words of support. She said that my physical symptoms did not yet require my hospitalization. She added that I could come any time, since the emotional aspects of a miscarriage can be more devastating than the physical ones. I was amazed but encouraged that someone recognized the emotional aspects of miscarriage and was willing to take professional time to deal with them. Realizing that I was in no physical danger, I remained at home and so was able to delay my hospitalization by another twenty-four hours.

At Queen's Medical Centre I was placed in the far corner of a gynecology ward in a private room, simply, but nicely, decorated with flowers on the windowsill. After my experience of spending the night in a crowded emergency ward during my first miscarriage, I was grateful for the privacy and that no one hurried to send me on my way again. The doctors did another ultrasound and decided to wait the night to see if the miscarriage would "complete itself naturally"—meaning they could avoid doing the "evacuation procedure." In the morning, however, they decided I should have the D&C to avoid a later infection. Because I was not an emergency case, I was put into a queue for the surgical "theatre" and finally had surgery that Saturday evening. They allowed me a night in the hospital to recuperate: a real blessing not having my two-year-old daughter waking me at five-thirty in the morning.

During my stay I saw several teams of doctors and was struck by their sincerity. Patient with our questions, thoughtful with their answers, never did they give the impression that I was "just another miscarriage." Even though I was depressed, I couldn't help smiling to myself when they kept referring to us women with miscarriages as "ladies"—a quaint term to American ears, but somehow respectful.

The nurses were also sympathetic, committed, and well-trained. This miscarriage was almost painless, with only occasional cramping, and I was able to go three days on the equivalent of two extra-strength, over-the-counter painkillers. Yet they often reminded me that I could have stronger medication if I needed it. Both my husband and I received discharge counseling and were invited to attend a service of "remembrance" for couples experiencing miscarriage, stillbirth, or infant death. One of the nurses also informed us that, unless we requested otherwise, the remains of our baby from the surgery would be cremated and placed in a "garden of remembrance" in a nearby cemetery. Though this idea was a bit foreign to us, and we could never see ourselves going to such a place, it was moving to us that life, even in its earlier stages, would be so revered.

After my discharge from the hospital, we really didn't have much time to think about the miscarriage because of the work demands and the sudden hospitalization of my father-in-law with a life-threatening illness the very next week. I must say that having a two-year-old was wonderfully distracting and made me more aware of how fortunate we were to have one child.

Three weeks later I did attend the service of remembrance, which allowed me time to grieve and to talk to a pastor, a nurse specialist in miscarriage, and other couples who had just experienced a loss. In the chapel there was a book of remembrance in which couples had recorded the date of their child's birth and death and any words of remembrance. Some of the entries were most stirring with their words of what it means to lose a child.

My follow-up appointment with my obstetrician was surprising. A specialist in pre-eclampsia, he noted that my miscarriage might have been prevented with a course of low-dose aspirin therapy. Our reaction to this news was mixed—hope, for a future pregnancy, frustration that no one had mentioned this treatment earlier. What a huge difference this experimental therapy might have made in our lives. Once again we attempted another pregnancy.

✳

June 1995—England

At the time of this writing, unfortunately, pregnancy is not happening and I am now in another period of adjustment. Part of me is accepting the idea of not being able to conceive again as I approach my fortieth birthday and as other problems in our ability to get pregnant become apparent. Just like in any grieving process, I've needed time to reach this point. On a recent family holiday, hiking in northern England and Scotland, I was inspired by the landscape around me and realized what I was missing by focusing too much on another pregnancy. I finally felt I had reached some degree of acceptance and serenity about our situation. Later that week, out of the blue, I heard that a friend from our first prenatal class had just delivered another baby and I burst into tears.

I expect these episodes of grieving will become less frequent since I am trying to accept whatever happens. One of the hard parts, I think, is that it's never really evident to people you meet that you have any problems with fertility or miscarriage, so people can quite innocently say things that are difficult. On another recent trip we stayed at a charming old farmhouse near the south coast of England and met a friendly couple who were pregnant with their third child, who was due very near when our baby would have been born. Of course, it was only polite to congratulate them and certainly socially unacceptable to tell them that I would have been delivering in July as well, had I not miscarried. They told us that they really hadn't planned this baby and were just looking forward to some freedom from babies—fertility was never a problem for them, they laughed. How could we say that it's been a horrible problem for us and that we would love to be having our third child? We just smiled, as if we understood, and eventually managed to turn the conversation to something more bearable.

I have met other women who have had miscarriages, of course. I have never felt the need to join a support group for miscarriage or infertility. Maybe I just don't want to let the problem take up this much of my life. My husband and I talk about adopting and, although our ages make it difficult, I am not ready to give up. I still have so many maternal instincts and I believe I'm meant to be a mother again. We remain in love with our two-year-old daughter, who seems totally unaware she's missing anything as an only child. Perhaps there is a plus side to problem pregnancies since you learn never to take your child or children for granted. And your joy is magnified if and when things go right.

As we prepare to return to the United States, we have much to do and little time to think about wanting another child. But part of me just wants to say good-bye to what might have been our living baby, strewn as ashes in a memorial garden in England.

HUMAN TIME

Jorie Miller

(For Mike and Katharine)

I know this third miscarriage is what causes you
to rest your head in your hand in that particular, weary way
while outside birds heckle the impatience you feel
with a springtime that has too much slow bleeding.

Katharine, impatience means nothing to the birds.
The sparrows circled again and again
when my neighbor dumped a nest
from the tarp covering his air conditioner.
The eggs smashed, revealing dark circles of eyes,
pasty wet feathers and slender necks.
The red, moist skins of the nearly-born birds
laid next to the fragments of pale blue shells.

My neighbor was sorry.
He held the nest made of thick twigs,
the inside lined with dryer lint, the finest soft grasses.
I gathered the small bodies,
scooped a hole under a not yet blooming spirea.
My five-year-old daughter brought
dandelions to line the grave.

We are sitting at the table with the lace tablecloth again,
waiting for summer, for heat, for flowers to grow.
We are waiting for eggs to hatch, for feathers to fluff,
for birds to fly away.
We are waiting for the life that comes after these deaths.

MISCARRIED MOURNING

Emily Martha Schultz

"I'm not upset about it and I don't want to talk about it," I said, after telling an old friend from college that I had just had a miscarriage. I had really called to make lunch plans with his wife—she and I have a long-standing tradition of taking each other out on our birthdays. It was unfortunate that her husband had answered the phone. I wanted to take care of business and then get on with what I had called about.

Oh, I knew that a miscarriage, no matter how early on in pregnancy, really is a loss. And that you have to mourn it. And that there's no way of putting yourself on a schedule which will tell you, by some objective measure, that you're finally over it. Beyond that knowledge, as a psychologist, I've always expressed belief in an eleventh commandment: know and experience your feelings. But despite all this expertise about feelings, this miscarriage was not going to affect me. I had one child, so was capable of getting pregnant and carrying a baby to term. I had had no trouble getting pregnant. My periods came every twenty-eight days like clockwork. So I'd just get pregnant again, that's all. Yes, sometimes I cried, despaired, and doubted my feminine capabilities, but wasn't I done with that now?

I'd had a similar reaction to my mother's death five years earlier. She had been horribly, inhumanly sick for six years. First, at age forty-five, she got Hodgkin's disease. Radiation and chemotherapy cured that, but as a result of the aggressive treatment, she got leukemia. She went through the hell of a bone marrow transplant. That involved three months of isolation and all kinds of known and unknown side effects, including paralysis. Then the leukemia came back, and nine months later, at fifty-one, she died. She'd had all of this, after never having had more than the flu before.

A distant relative remarked to one of my brothers that I "looked very unaffected" at my mother's funeral. Although it hurt to hear about this comment, it was probably true. I repeated to myself the things that other people said to me: "She was sick for so long," "She suffered so much," "You knew she was going to die," and "Maybe now she's found some peace." At least now I could grieve, instead of continually hoping for her to do better, or wanting for there to be some new miracle treatment, or waiting for her to die. Except I never really did grieve. Weren't all those things that people said true? Wasn't I relieved?

My mother and I never got to be adults together. Although I was twenty-eight when she died, we had only just begun to sort out all of those mother-daughter adolescent feelings about separation, disappointment, and rebellion. I was just beginning to learn that it was all right to do things my own way, even if that disappointed her, and even if that pleased her. It was fairly new news that although she might fret and nag and needle and prod, she was not going to hate me, or even dislike me, for not choosing the house with the white picket fence. She would always be there for me—until she got sick and died.

My mother and I played out different roles in the same family drama. My mother's father, Edward Marget, died suddenly of a heart attack at the age of forty-six, when she was fifteen. When it came to Edward Marget, it seemed that my mother never lost the awe and reverence a little girl has for her father. Throughout my childhood, I heard about this brilliant, handsome, musical, funny, cultured, Harvard-educated man whom I would never know. The few references my mother made to my grandfather being a little tyrannical and moody, somehow, only added to the wondrous portrait she painted of him.

I did not idealize my mother. For too many years, I hung onto that complicated, sometimes obnoxious, way teenage girls treat their mothers. She was always one of the first people I ran to with good news or bad, for rejoicing or comfort, or so I could say, "I told you so." I used my mother to learn the lesson that you can fight and be horrible and say things you don't mean, but when there is a fundamental connection, the person will always be there. Given how often I tested her, I was a slow learner. There were enough unresolved issues between us that when she died, it was hard for me to allow myself to feel the terrible loss.

After my mother's death, I forged ahead with many of the things I had always wanted for myself. The sequel to my warm and elegant wedding, which she masterminded from her sickbed, is a deeply gratifying marriage that only gets better with time. We have a beautiful son, who is named after his maternal grandmother. I am happy and successful in my career.

Then the miscarriage happened. Although many pregnancies end in miscarriage, I had never thought it would happen to me. That's partly why I didn't want to talk about it with my college friend's husband on the phone or with anyone else. I didn't let the miscarriage bother me and I was just going to move on to the next thing, getting back on the invulnerable track I had signed up for as if it were honors classes in high school. I did find myself worrying about a million unrelated things, from the pens and checkbooks I kept misplacing to the effect of passive smoking. But everything was just fine.

What changed my attitude was an unexpected day off work. I arrived at my office to find all the doors to the building locked because of Evacuation Day, an obscure holiday celebrated only in one county of Massachusetts. Somehow, in the midst of everything being fine, I had failed to notice that we were given a day off. "Everyone else got it," I found myself saying on the way home, which is what I used to say when I stumbled over high school math. After getting over the disruption this caused to my compulsively planned schedule, I decided it was a chance to catch up on some long overdue errands. I had been meaning to buy my father and his fiancée a housewarming gift. I decided to go to a gourmet food store in the neighboring town where I grew up. My mother used to go there a lot. She'd send care packages from the shop to my brothers and me when we were at summer camp; at college; and living in that weird, post-student, transitional phase in our twenties. I almost fell asleep at the wheel on the short drive there.

Although I had loved the cheeses, nuts, cookies, and jams that came in those care packages, I had never shopped at the store. Fighting my fatigue, I busied myself, selecting coffee beans and chutneys. I had never felt more like my mother. I decided to ask the people helping me how long they had worked there. "Oh, we've had the store about fifteen years," the man said. Well, that was certainly long enough to have known my mother, I thought. "Well, I'm asking because I'm wondering if you knew Roberta Schultz—I'm her daughter," I said. "Oh, yes, she came in here all the time. She was always sending packages to you and your brothers. She'd spend a lot of time making sure we had all the apartment numbers right." Don't cry, don't cry, don't cry, don't cry. I cleared my throat and said, "Yes, we all loved those pack-ages." He said, "I can see her."

Though grateful for this tacit shared appreciation of who my mother was, I ran out of the store. I got home and cried. I wanted that baby, I missed my mother, and I wanted to share the experi-ence of being a mother with my mother. And I wanted my mother to tell me everything would be all right.

WADING THROUGH TIME

Keith Kuenning

I knew you only
by the twinkle of your heart
but the twinkle stopped

now
I am just wading through time
burdened by life
and surrounded by grief
pulled down
by death's undertow

sometimes
I feel like not fighting the pull
to let go
and come to you

someday
I hope
the pain will leave
and that all that will be left
is the love

yet
I know
the pain of your loss
will never—
completely—
be gone.

BRANDEN AND KEVIN

LaDawna Lawton

Shortly after buying our first home, my husband and I adopted a puppy from a stray's litter. On Baxter's first night home, he seemed ill. After several trips to the vet, we learned he had distemper. After being a member of our family for only two weeks, Baxter died. "If we are this upset over losing a puppy, can you imagine what it must be like to lose a baby?" I asked my husband. I have no idea what made me say that. I never even knew anyone who had. And when I said those words, I never dreamed we'd ever really find out.

Steve and I always wanted children, but when the test turned pink, it came as a surprise. We were excited about having a baby, but being the planners we are, doubts set in. Did we have enough money? Were we ready? I even wondered if I would be jealous of the baby's relationship with Steve since he'd be such a great father. And was he! He immediately wanted to decorate the nursery. Being cautious, I advised we wait until after the first trimester. "It would upset me to have a nursery ready if I had a miscarriage," I said. So, when I hit twelve weeks we started the renovations.

I had the perfect pregnancy; I never even threw up. I was in my twenties and the doctors rushed me in and out of the prenatal visits, telling me I was the picture of good health. They assured me that, statistically, I was at the best age to have a healthy baby. When at my thirty-one week checkup, I complained of terrible back pain, the nurse-practitioner said, as she chuckled, "Honey, that's what it's like to be pregnant." Three days later, I was leaking amniotic fluid and contracting every two to three minutes. After several attempts to delay labor, it became necessary to deliver.

Our son, Branden Louis Lawton, was born at thirty-two weeks gestation. As soon as the doctor cleared his airway, he let out the most beautiful sound we had ever heard. He cried, which meant he was able to breathe. Steve and I cried joyfully as we watched our little boy being cleaned up. A nurse brought Branden, wrapped snugly in a blanket and a hat on his head, to me to hold before she whisked him away to the neonatal intensive care unit. When he looked at me with his tiny blue eyes, it was the happiest moment of my life.

At 3 pounds, 9.5 ounces and 17 inches, Branden was one of the largest babies in the care unit. He was doing well, required no additional oxygen, and was expected to go home in approximately six weeks. Steve and I visited our baby boy daily; we held him, took pictures, and looked forward to bringing him home.

When Branden was two days old, they told us he had a minor heart murmur, but it was nothing to be concerned about. We were horribly surprised when, on the sixth day, they informed us he would need corrective surgery. We went home for dinner and notified our families of this shocking news. When we returned, we were greeted with even worse news: Branden had developed a life-threatening intestinal infection. We stayed several hours; the visit was very sad. Heartbroken, we watched our son as he lay moaning in pain. The doctor suggested we go home to rest and assured us he'd call if anything changed.

As soon as we got home, the phone rang. Our son's condition had worsened. Emergency surgery revealed that the infection had progressed to the point where Branden could not be saved. Prior to surgery, he had been placed on a respirator, so we were faced with the agonizing decision of removing him from life-support. Branden died fifteen minutes later; he was seven days old.

I am sad to say, we were not with him when he died. It is a decision I will regret for the rest of my life, but, I know now, we made the best decision we could at that time. We would do it differently, if we could go back, but we cannot.

One year later, on the anniversary of Branden's funeral, his sister Kaitlen Louise was born. She will never replace her brother, but she fills our home with laughter and our hearts with love, and she has taught us how to smile again.

✳

In October of 1994, I became pregnant again. This baby was to be our third child, a living sibling for Kaitlen and a gift of hope for my grandmother, who is terminally ill with lung cancer.

My husband and I had chosen the ideal age difference between our children and, after having been successful with Kaitlen, this pregnancy seemed manageable. Naturally, we did have fears; how could we not after experiencing the death of our baby? We picked out names and gave the baby in my womb an important place in our family. We made plans.

At five weeks, I had cramping and a show of blood. Since I had never bled before, I was concerned and phoned the doctor. He had me come in for an ultrasound—it showed "a perfect five week sac with good implantation." Still concerned, I went home feeling a little more reassured.

My next prenatal visit was at nine weeks. It was routine: blood pressure, step-on-the-scale, and pee-in-a-cup. I left feeling upset and concerned about the baby. I told my husband, "They don't even know if the baby is alive or dead."

At ten weeks I began to feel very nervous. I spoke to a friend and told her how I was feeling. She suggested I call my doctor, but I brushed it off, telling her that it was probably just "subsequent pregnancy jitters."

On Saturday, December 10th, I was lying on the couch, eleven weeks pregnant, sick with a cold, watching a video of *Charlotte's Web* with my daughter. Suddenly, I felt some discharge. I thought about my friend who had four miscarriages and how she would have panicked at such a feeling, and considered myself lucky for never having been through such an experience. About thirty minutes later, I got up to use the bathroom. I was horrified to find that I had bled through my pajamas. I panicked, but managed to phone my doctor; his partner was on call. When his partner called me back, he advised me to stay in bed. I felt alone.

My bleeding continued. On Sunday night the blood loss became heavier and bright red and I was cramping. My husband decided to take me to the nearest hospital. The emergency room doctor could not locate a heartbeat and ordered a HCG—human chorionic gonadotrophin—count. He wanted me to stay, so I could have a D&C if needed, but I refused. He called our house an hour later with the results of the blood test. The HCG level was extremely low. The doctor recommended we call the obstetrician in the morning to schedule the D&C.

We had recently moved, so I was alone with no friends, no other family and a new obstetrician I didn't know well. The doctor who had delivered Kaitlen was also my friend, so I called her early Monday morning. She told me to demand an ultrasound so I could know for certain if the baby had died.

Later that day the ultrasound showed the baby was dead. As I left the hospital after the D&C, a nurse wheeled me past the "Family Birth Center" and I watched a mother leaving with a healthy baby. I was leaving with nothing. I never felt my baby move, never heard the baby's heartbeat, and was refused a picture of my dead baby.

One of the hardest things to deal with after my miscarriage was the lack of recognition from family and friends. When Branden died, people sent flowers, cards, and donations to help with expenses. This time there was little support. People made comments like, "It was only a miscarriage," "At least it happened now, instead of like Branden," and "There was probably something wrong with the baby." Only a few were there for us: a group of friends sent us a "Fragrant Memory" rosebush and a dear friend sent us a houseplant, two keepsakes I treasure.

The losses of Branden Louis and Kevin Lynzi were very different. Each loss had characteristics that made it easier in some ways and harder in others. Kevin Lynzi was as much a part of me as Branden and Kaitlen. Only this time, I do not have a face to put with the love I carry for my child.

*

I am now fifteen weeks pregnant with our fourth baby. I am not enjoying this pregnancy. I just want to get to the end and bring home a healthy child. Although this is not the script I had written for our family, we have somehow managed. Steve and I have a strong relationship. Kaitlen is happy and healthy and we are honest with her. At two and a half, she knows about Branden and Kevin, as will our next baby, provided we make it that far.

My advice to women experiencing a pregnancy loss is this: always try to be honest with your partner about your feelings and try to respect his—even if they are very different from your own. Be honest with your children; they are smarter than you think. And remember, too, that you are stronger than you think you are. You can make it through this and return to some sense of normalcy. I know it's not fair. But, as I tell Kaitlen, "Life isn't always fair and you just have to deal with what you get."

FEBRUARY SIXTEENTH

Dylan Ann Treall

Here it is.
February sixteenth.
I thought I might cry.
I thought I wouldn't want to see any
    newborns
      remembering the one I didn't have.
But instead, I'm preparing to go on a women's retreat
    for a weekend
      feeling joy and excited anticipation.
I think instead of the healing I have done
    and what I know now,
      more of me.
I think of the ski season I did not miss
    and dancing
      and cream liqueur on New Year's.
I appreciate the freedom of my body.

Am I happy I'm not nine months huge now?
Am I relieved I don't have a newborn?
I cried for months.
Felt empty, hollow
I thought I would cry
    forever.
Should I feel guilty because
    I feel glad?
No.
I am living in the moment
    accepting my past
      my journey.

I am grateful for my learning
   my growth
   my understanding of self.

It is February sixteenth.
I plant a lilac bush under the
   bedroom window.
And continue to prepare for my retreat.
I would rather prepare for a birth.
I would rather have
My baby.

EXCERPTS FROM A PREGNANCY LOSS JOURNAL

Deborah McCleary

Monday, April 25, 1988

Miracle of miracles—I am pregnant! David and I can hardly believe it. Thank you, God. Thank you, thank you, thank you. We will try to do everything right—exactly what the doctor tells us. Our first GIFT worked! (GIFT stands for gamete intrafallopian transfer; it is similar to in vitro fertilization but with a few different twists.) It turns out that I hold the record for the number of eggs produced by a GIFT patient—seventeen—and one of them got zapped.

*

Sunday, May 8, 1988

Mother's Day—that means me, too. I even got a few cards for the expectant mother. For the first time in a few years I'll be able to go to church and feel part of it on this day.

*

Sunday, May 15, 1988

We visited David's parents today. When Mom and I were shopping, suddenly I felt a warm discharge, like I was bleeding. I ran into the house and sure enough, I was bleeding, bright red. This kept up for a couple of hours. It wasn't oodles of blood, but it was enough to scare me. I don't want to lose this baby! I just can't imagine that—to be given such a precious gift, literally and figuratively, and then lose that wonderful life. Please don't let that happen, God.

*

Sunday, May 29, 1988

I have been bleeding intermittently for the past two weeks. I've almost gotten used to the brown discharge, but the bright red makes me so uneasy. I shouldn't worry, but today I am depressed and beside myself. After church I cried for about two hours, for no good reason, which is not like me. I suppose it's hormonal, but I can't shake the feeling that something is radically wrong with this pregnancy.

I don't want anything to happen to the baby. My mother lost four babies and I am terrified that I could repeat her misfortune. Her doctor told her that her problem was hormonal.

I have to get a grip on myself. I know it's not good for the baby for me to be upset. It is so hard to rein in my emotions, though. I feel unable to stifle my brain and its racing, fearful thoughts.

*

Tuesday, May 31, 1988

I've been unable to shake this feeling of foreboding, so I decided to seek a second opinion after I see my doctor. I got an appointment with a friend's doctor for Friday. He'll probably say that I'm over-reacting and that everything is fine. I trust my doctor, but it never hurts to get another opinion. If only I could shake off these negative feelings.

*

Thursday, June 2, 1988

I questioned my beta level today because I feel it hasn't risen appropriately. The nurse suggested I come in for an ultrasound the next morning. When I asked why, she said to see how many babies I had. This seems odd, because we already know I only have one, but I'll go—no problem.

I guess tomorrow will really be doctor morning. Then we take off for a short vacation with family. I just don't feel right about everything.

✳

Friday, June 3, 1988

What a horrible day. My beta level is falling. The ultrasound didn't pick up a heartbeat; it looks like this pregnancy is doomed. I can hardly believe it. I feel like I've been kicked in the stomach and all over my body. I'm in a state of shock and yet, intuitively, I know it's true.

My precious baby, so hard-earned, is not going to be. Why God, why? I don't understand. I asked my friend's doctor if he was sure; he said that if the beta level turned around there was a slight possibility that everything would be okay, but he was doubtful.

✳

Friday, June 10, 1988

Our vacation was awful. I was in a state of shock and could not get my mind off my body and the baby I was losing. I walked around with cups in my purse to catch any discharge, should I begin to miscarry—which I didn't. I think David was thankful to get home, just to get a break from me. I can't say I blame him.

My beta level definitely dropped yesterday. I went in for an ultrasound and I said I knew it would be bad news. The doctor looked at the picture and said I was right. The baby was no longer there.

We tentatively scheduled a D&C for Tuesday, June 14. That seems like a long time away, but it was the best we could do. I am anxious to get tissue for analysis. Did this baby have Down's syndrome or trisomy 13 or what? I want to know. My doctor said most likely it is the one in five chance of loss there is with every pregnancy, but why this one when we'd worked so hard? It doesn't seem fair. I suppose, if a pregnancy has to be lost, the earlier, the better, but it doesn't feel that way right now. I want my baby back and I can't have him or her back. Why does it hurt so much? There are so many lost hopes and dreams. But we will try again, and maybe next time, we'll have our baby. At least we know we can conceive and that's something to go on.

*

Wednesday, June 15, 1988

A day for good-byes. I didn't sleep well last night. I just kept thinking that our long-awaited baby was gone and how much that hurt. A dark cloud is hanging over me and I hope when we try again, we'll not have this disappointment. I think, though, if it could happen once, it could happen again. But it won't, right?

My D&C had to be moved to today because the doctor was caught in emergency surgery. At lunch time David called me and told me that his grandfather had just died. Although we knew it was coming, it seemed more than coincidental on this momentous day. Now our baby and his or her great-grandfather will be traveling together. In a strange way that is comforting. The doctor was able to remove the entire egg sac, which was good. He told me to get a blood test immediately, just to make sure I do not have an RH factor problem. It will take four to six weeks to get the results from the D&C. That seems so long and I want some answers. I only hope that we didn't wait too long to do the D&C. I know it seems premature, but I want to try to conceive again tomorrow.

*

Friday, June 17, 1988

It was strange to have to ignore our pain, but we had to because of Pop's death. Dad said he knew we were hurting, but I said that even though we were, we had to first deal with our loss of Pop. We'll deal with us and the lost baby later, but I still feel so empty.

*

Tuesday, June 21, 1988

I had a post-D&C checkup today. The doctor asked me how I was doing emotionally and I said I was doing much better because I had anticipated the loss.

This empty feeling will continue for a while. I feel so sad and put upon. It's bad enough to deal with loss, but when it is coupled with a procedure where you tried so hard to conceive, it seems to add insult to injury. Why God, why? I don't understand, but will I ever?

*   *   *

Monday, July 18, 1988

I am anxious to prepare for another GIFT. I'm running away from my grief and yet the only way I feel I have a chance to conceive is to put us on the line again. I don't want to waste any time.

*

Since our first loss, David and I have lost four other children: at six weeks, at eight weeks, at twenty weeks, and a twin at ten weeks. I have also given birth to two sons. Christopher, the twin's brother, was born in 1991 and Trevor was born in 1993.

David and I spent so many years investing our emotions, time, energy, and money in trying to have children that it feels odd to bring this chapter of our lives to a close. When I look at Trevor's tiny face and Christopher's big blue eyes, however, I know that everything we went through was worth it. I would do it all again to bring these boys into our lives.

BABY OF MY OWN

Cindy Steines

"Baby My-O, the sun is warm. This is a good day, oh baby of my own."

I spoke out loud sometimes, but most times the words did not pass my lips, but were sent instead through some yet-to-be-discovered message way directly to my baby. Each day as my belly became more rotund, I was determined to share my thoughts and experiences with this person developing within me. I wanted to enjoy the relationship that only the two of us could know. In this my fourth pregnancy, I did not assume that there would always be another day of life.

When I first experienced pregnancy over twenty years ago, I was scared. Perhaps it was because my sister had just died in her prime, lost to cancer. Or maybe it was low self-esteem that led me to think that I could never do anything so wonderful as create life. Or maybe it was just the same unnerving disbelief any mother-to-be might feel when trying to understand the concept of a new life taking shape within her. I had worried thoughts. Could this really be happening? Could something go wrong? Could it go away as quickly as it had begun? I waited almost three months before I told anyone but my husband. Just after that, I began to feel sick. I lay for several days feeling weak and nauseated before the labor-like pains began. For three more days, in the hospital, I worried and wondered before I knew for sure that the pregnancy was over.

What an emptiness I knew after that. How could I explain my low feelings, my unfulfilled longings, my disoriented sense of loss? I wasn't even sure what it was that I had lost. I did not yet know what it was like to be a mother. I had never had the chance to bond with a new baby or to fully understand what the miracle of life really was. For me, miscarriage was failing at life and finding despair.

Pregnancy came again to me and this time I hardly dared to feel or think about it through the first months. I did not always feel well and I worried constantly about every discomfort that I had. But when those first weeks had passed and my belly began to swell, I started to believe, with reservation, that it could be all right this time. I felt more sure of myself and more excited as the weeks passed. After carrying full term, I delivered, with relative ease, a baby boy. When they first brought Benjamin to me in my room, late in the evening, I found within me a depth of feeling that I had never before known. The bond that began was unlike any other. I made commitments in that deepest part of me to love, to care for, and to be prepared to give my own life for the tiny being I held in my arms. I was beginning to know what it was like to be a mother. Later, I fell asleep a new, richer person.

Soon I awoke to strange inquiries from the nurses about family medical history and the pregnancy. I began to feel uneasy, and when I spoke to the doctor, I had a sense of foreboding. The doctor said that the baby had problems and would be sent immediately to a neonatal center in a major hospital in a bigger city. No one knew what was wrong with Benjamin and they wondered if they should baptize him before he left the hospital.

Words cannot convey my anxiety and despair. That the heights of joy and happiness could so soon be twisted into pain-filled hours seemed unbelievable. When might I have had more reason to be filled with hope than when I held my newborn infant? I had let every feeling I had be touched by this baby. What was this life that could be given and perhaps taken away so quickly?

A week later, all the worry and tears, the calls to the hospital, the painful milk-filled breasts that fed no baby, and the sleepless nights were rewarded with the best news. Benjamin was recovering and had the promise of a very normal life. I did have a baby, my son, to take home with me.

But in my third pregnancy I miscarried again. That very morning I had told the news of the pregnancy for the first time. Hours later, I thought it was over. How tenuous is this living condition.

How indiscriminate the gift of life, and pain of loss. I was not able to know this life: my child lost in its earliest stages.

But I had another chance. In my fourth pregnancy the first weeks were unsure once again. In the later weeks, when I began to feel life within me as the baby grew, I became determined to enjoy this wondrous condition. Who could know when it might be over? Too soon? If I didn't miscarry, this baby might have a life-threatening condition at birth as Benjamin had. I wanted to share my love with this being every day I could. I couldn't be sure there would be another day, another chance, so I talked with Baby My-O, sharing the pleasures of my life. There is no promise of tomorrow. We have this day, this time, to share and to enjoy. Throughout the pregnancy, I enjoyed as best I could the life within.

Baby My-O came into the world easily enough. But in circumstances identical to my son's, she had to have immediate treatment for a serious condition. Rebecca did come home a healthy baby, though, and I think how fortunate I am to have two healthy children.

To be a woman and be able to carry a baby is a wondrous thing. The capacity to nurture and love is also the capacity to feel the pain of loss. Pregnancy is a time to develop a deeper understanding of yourself and to enjoy the life within. Pregnancy—a time of uncertainty and sometimes death of the child—is a time to turn your face to the sun and say, "It is a fine day to be alive, Baby of My Own."

PATTERN

Evelyn Fielding

Since you've been gone...
I've marked each lilac dawn,
each blooming harvest moon;
when twilight slips
cold hands in mine
I dream the quilted puzzle
of our lives—
You leave me always
when days grow cold,
heartbeats stilled,
pattern unbroken.
Death? No,
but purgatory,
neither heaven nor hell,
just silence, awaiting
winter and your return...

THE BOX IN THE CLOSET: THOUGHTS ON MY DUE DATE

Carla Sofka

There is a box in the closet.

Inside the box, there is a tiny outfit made of snow-white cloth. Bright green threads stitched on the front proclaim a momentous occasion: Baby's First Christmas.

But there is so much more in that box in the closet.

It carries remnants of our hope, our plans, and anticipation of the holidays with our first baby. Our parents were eager to come to upstate New York in winter, the dread of snow and cold set aside to visit a new grandchild. We would laugh, smile, talk in silly voices, and make those funny faces that appear when a baby is in a room lit by Christmas lights.

The box carries my memories of preparation. I remember going to the baby section at a big department store during the end-of-winter sale. "You'll need these to keep the baby warm in winter," the clerk said. "You'll be glad that you bought them now—they'll be very expensive when you need them."

There were snowsuits for miniature people—material so soft and warm, and covered with bears, dinosaurs, balloons, and stars. "How much does a two-and-a-half-month-old baby weigh?" I asked. "What size will I need when the baby is that age?" I inquired. I wondered what it would be like to try to get my squirming baby into a snowsuit and zip it up.

Today I am reminded of that box in the closet.

This is the day that Jason or Carrie was supposed to be born. Those brightly stitched threads still proclaim a momentous occasion—but one that won't happen this year.

Illogical but powerful thoughts overwhelm me: I should not have bought anything so early; if only I would have waited, the baby would be here. I must have jinxed my pregnancy by getting too excited. Why did I keep this Christmas outfit? A voice in my heart reminds me that I just could not take this one back.

This box makes me cry. I imagine a Christmas filled with emptiness, even though I will not be alone. There will be no toys around the Christmas tree. I will hang two stockings instead of three. I will hear holiday music, but I fear unbearable silence—a silence noticed only by me. There will not be coos, gurgles, hunger cries, or baby talk. Will there be laughter on Christmas Day?

There is a box in the closet filled with bittersweet memories of creating a life and experiencing a new life inside; it is also filled with the grief and pain of losing a baby.

There is a box in the closet that some day will be filled again with hope.

MY FIVE CHILDREN

Lori Watts

I have had five children, not just two. I lost Benjamin in 1981 when he was about twenty weeks. I was twenty-one years old. I lost Sarah in 1984 when she was about sixteen weeks. In 1990, I lost Allison who, like the others, was too small to survive.

After losing two babies I didn't know if I wanted to try to become pregnant any more. I didn't know if I could go through the heartache of losing another child. But on August 1, 1985, I found out I was going to have a baby. I had mixed feelings and wasn't sure I wanted to be pregnant. My husband Scott, though, was excited. He was sure that this baby was going to live; he set the crib up that night.

He knew what he was talking about because on March 30, 1986, Easter Sunday, our daughter Amy was born. She was a beautiful healthy baby and her birth made me hope for another child soon. People told me I probably wouldn't have any more miscarriages. Their words were encouraging because I had always wanted four living children.

Four years later I became pregnant, but lost the baby. Because I already had a child, people tried to comfort me by saying, "You should be thankful you have Amy" or "Be thankful you have a child because some people don't have any." These words did not help me; the words hurt me. Wanting another child didn't mean I wasn't thankful to have Amy.

Two years after our third loss, on August 14, 1992, our son Adam was born. I was happy and relieved. My maternal feelings were strong, however, and still I yearned for more children. While pregnant with Adam, though, I developed heart problems and my doctors advised me not to have another baby. This was like having another miscarriage. The choice of having more children was taken away from me.

As Adam became older, I became depressed. I did a lot of unexplained crying. All I had to do was look at Adam and I would start to cry. I found myself constantly looking at Adam's baby pictures and videos. I couldn't understand my emotions. I should have been happy. After all, I had a wonderful husband and two healthy children. What was happening to me?

Months later I read an article in the local newspaper about a group called HEARTS (Helping Empty Arms Recover Through Sharing), a support group for parents who have lost a child or children through miscarriage, stillbirth, neonatal death or ectopic pregnancy. I found the answer: I had lost three babies and was never allowed to grieve. I longed for the babies and couldn't try to have the four living children I'd hoped for.

The article told about how the group helped people like me. It welcomed new members and listed a phone number. After a lot of crying, I picked up the phone and dialed the number. Neither of the co-facilitators—a woman who'd lost a baby through miscarriage and a woman who was an obstetrics nurse—were in the office. The operator gave me the nurse's home number. Again no answer. I left word on the answering machine for the nurse to call me when she could. That night she called and I told her my story. We talked a long time and I cried. After I hung up, I felt better.

Without realizing it, I was starting to grieve for my babies. This was an important step in my healing process. About half an hour after the nurse and I finished talking, the other group leader called. Again I cried and told my story. Both women were caring and understanding. Never once did they make me feel I was wrong for the feelings I had, even though the babies had died years ago. The next day, both women called to make sure I was all right.

Several more phone calls led me to the HEARTS group. I met others who had lost babies and I felt a sense of comfort, that I wasn't the only one experiencing so much pain. It helped me to talk with other parents. It didn't matter if the baby was lost a long time ago or recently. We were all there to tell our stories to those who understood and to share ideas about dealing with the pain. Different people grieve in different ways; there is no wrong or right way to grieve.

Because of the group's support, I decided to have a memorial service for my babies. Since many years had elapsed between the deaths of my children—Benjamin had died over ten years before—and the memorial service, I had plenty of time to do things the way I wanted. Because I was afraid that some people would react in an unsupportive way, I decided to plan the memorial before I told anyone outside the HEARTS group. That way no one could talk me out of having it. The HEARTS co-facilitators helped me get in touch with a funeral home. The funeral director listened to my ideas and helped me make the arrangements with the cemetery. My pastor was also receptive and helped me plan the memorial service. Having made these arrangements, I told other people who I felt would understand why this service was important for me.

During this time I had still not told my husband about the support group or about the memorial service. I was nervous about his reaction. Whenever I had tried to talk to him before, he would tell me I needed to get on with my life. One evening while we were making dinner I told him. He said that if the memorial service would make me feel better he would totally support me. We then talked about the babies. His belief was that the miscarriages were meant to be. He also said that he understood how I felt about the babies and that I should understand he had a right to feel his way.

After telling Scott, I decided to tell a few other people about the service. Unlike when the babies died, everyone I told was supportive. The HEARTS group gave me a small casket to bury. My mother helped me sew a white satin lining with a lovely heart for the inside of the casket. We then put in three bears, each holding a heart with the name of one of the babies. My mother had made three pairs of tiny booties. They were pink, blue, and yellow; each color represented one of my babies. We put the booties in the casket along with our family picture. I wrote a poem to use as a temporary marker for the grave and my father helped me make a weatherproof frame.

On July 12, 1993, we had the memorial service. While the poem I had written was read, I released three balloons. Benjamin was written on one, Sarah was written on one, and Allison was written on one. I had purchased a small casket-spray of red carnations interspersed with four white carnations representing Scott, Amy, Adam and me. I placed three carnations—pink, blue, and yellow—on the casket to be buried with the remembrances of the babies. I then said good-bye to my three dead children.

My sister took the bouquet of flowers she had given for the memorial service to be frozen and dried, to preserve their colors. She placed them, along with other memorabilia, in a glass globe. All of these things, as well as pictures of the service, help keep alive the memory of my babies.

My crying has lessened with time. The pain and desire to have more children is still there, but not as strong. I am happy with the family I have. And what I have done has helped me in the healing process.

STONE BOY

Barbara Santucci

Stone statue,
My wingless angel.

My son's face,
Locked in the grave of my mind.

The one constant
In the blur of my busy days.

Stone Boy, anchored to the ground,
Motionless.

My son, entombed in the earth,
Motionless.

His soft flesh turned cold,
Like yours.

Angels dance around the face of Jesus,
Who awaits him.

His spirit rises
In waves of red that reach the sun.

Together we gaze out
At the glowing western sky.

OUR THREE MISCARRIAGES

Stuart Johnston

My wife, Carol, and I have experienced three miscarriages: one before the birth of our daughter, Katie, and two after her birth. All three losses were different, physically and emotionally.

The first miscarriage started at work—we work in the same building but in different offices—in the afternoon. I left my office and was startled to see a frightened look on my wife's face as she walked toward the bathroom. That's how I found out. This miscarriage lasted over two weeks and it was like a deathwatch for the two of us. At least six times a day I asked Carol how much spotting she had, if she felt any cramps, and, if so, how strong they were. We were seeing a doctor, but there was not much he could tell us, except that the pregnancy was "viable but threatened." Eventually, the fetus died and Carol "passed the tissue" (interesting terminology). It was almost a relief that it was over. I didn't have to check Carol for bleeding or cramps and we could put our lives back into some kind of order.

The second miscarriage was this past fall. After about a year of discussing whether or not we should have another child, a sibling for Katie, I decided I was okay with it. (I was the one who was not sure that I wanted another child.) We conceived right away and after knowing for about a week or so, Carol started bleeding. We had our second miscarriage. This one was much shorter but still painful. It had taken us so long to get to that place.

After the second miscarriage, we decided to wait a while and then try again. When we tried, we conceived right away and were excited. We were relieved when we made it past the first three months because that was when our other miscarriages had occurred. On a Thursday, though, Carol started spotting and we went to see the doctor. After an ultrasound, we found out the baby had died at about ten weeks into the pregnancy. We wanted to have the pregnancy end "procedurally" and made an appointment to see our regular doctor on Wednesday. We never got to that appointment. At one o'clock early Sunday morning I was awakened by the sound of fluid gushing in the bathroom. I thought Carol was getting sick, but instead she was bleeding. After calling the hospital, I arranged for a friend to stay in the house with Katie. What happened at the hospital was horrible. Carol was in great pain and passing blood clots the size of grapefruits. This went on until close to noon when the surgical team did an emergency D&C. Carol spent the next day in the hospital.

I have many feelings about our miscarriages. When I look at Katie and think that she is our "second" child, I wonder what would have happened to her if we had not miscarried the first time. The idea that she would not be here is very scary. I think that when you miscarry, you lose the body of the person, but not the soul, and that Katie's soul was waiting to be born. That's about as positive as I can be.

What frustrates me is when people say things like, "Well, it's nature's way of saying that something was wrong," or "It's God's will," or "You can have more." It is amazing that people, including medical staff, say things like this to make people who've lost a child feel better. God would not do this to my wife three times. I believe that bad things happen to good people and that life is not always fair. What I want explained to me—though nobody can— is why us, three times? We are young, healthy people who did everything right in caring for our unborn children. When people say "You can have more," do they think about what they are saying? It's not as if I lost a sock and I can just go get another one. Maybe I don't want to have another one.

I met with our doctor while Carol was still in the hospital and told him I didn't want to put my wife through a loss again, ever. I saw blood pouring out of my wife—my best friend, the most important person in my life, the person I care about deeply—for over seven hours as she screamed and wept from the exams and the pain. It's difficult to justify risking that again to have another child. I would have a hard time forgiving myself for putting my wife through that a fourth time.

The medical talk is about "procedures" and "tissue," but a miscarriage is a death. I have lost three children. I have mourned those deaths, some took longer than others, but each is still a death and each is still a loss. I have heard plenty of stories like, "I know someone who had four miscarriages and then had a healthy baby." That's fine for that person, but not for me.

I love my daughter and it has been very hard to tell her, twice, that the baby in Mommy's tummy died and she doesn't have a little brother or sister anymore. The last time I told her she said, "Well, Mommy could have another baby in her tummy." I said, "We may not want to do that again." She said, "Is it because you and Mommy are afraid that the baby might die again?" I said, "Yes, that's right, Katie." Coming from a four-year-old child, that's pretty perceptive.

Our three miscarriages have hurt me tremendously, though I don't compare it to what Carol has felt because she has had to live through the physical and the emotional pain. Carol is the only one who can really know what that has been like. Fathers who look forward to a child, and then lose that child, feel the loss and they grieve. Men *are* affected by miscarriages—whether they say it out loud or not.

As a community, we need to allow both parents—the mother and the father—to express how they feel. We cannot assume that everyone who has lost a child or children in miscarriage will feel the same.

NURSING THE UNBORN

Deborah Vaughan

Like
Swollen dumb mouths
Opening—

Like
Sore blind eyes
Weeping—

Ripe with bounty
Flowing—
For

One

Who can never drink.

FIFTEEN YEARS

Donna S. Frary

After fifteen years, sometimes it's hard for me to remember my miscarriage. Sometimes I think, to try to remember. Sometimes I feel, to try to remember. A word from someone, a scene in a movie, or a paragraph in a book sometimes brings the miscarriage back surprisingly strong and real.

✳

When I think, to try to remember, it seems like a story I heard someone tell. "You know a friend of mine miscarried. It's pretty common, they say. The doctor said one in five pregnancies ends in miscarriage." When I think, I am forever a one—a number—in the statistic.

When I think, I wonder about the word *miscarriage* and what it implies. Carrying something is an action a woman engages in, seems to have control over.

"Can you carry that into the house for me? Be careful, don't drop it!"

Does having a miscarriage mean I did something wrong in how I carried my child? When I carried other things and they weren't situated correctly, I could usually set them down, rearrange them, and pick them up again.

I can get philosophical when I think, to try to remember.

✳

When I feel, the memory of my miscarriage is clear and real. I barely had the chance to get used to the idea of a child. I was nineteen, not married, and unsure whether I wanted to be a mother. Although I loved the baby's father, the marriage issue was difficult. We weren't ready.

When I feel, I remember the spotting, the early cramping, and the fear. I feel the guilt that came just as I got excited about this new life, this possibility, this child.

What did I do wrong? I fell on the ice; was that the cause? Was I on my feet too much at work? What did I do?

When I feel, I remember the night of loss: the painful cramping, the seemingly long walk from the car to the emergency room entrance, and then the comfort of the warmed blanket the nurse thoughtfully put over me.

When I feel, sometimes it is pain and fear mixed together, as the contractions continued and the blood began. The tests were taken and in my heart I started to know.

I am still proud of my strength as I spoke with the doctor, hearing his news of a fetus no longer living. I'm proud of my strength as I made medical decisions. My strength was there until I called home to maturely inform my parents. At the concerned sound of my father's voice, I became his exhausted little girl who really did not want to be an adult.

When I feel, I recall the looks of love, the words of support, and faces of particular people who cared for and about me when I was out of surgery, recovering, and going home.

Mostly, though, when I feel, I recall the emptiness, the no feeling, and the numbness that stayed with me for days until the phone conversation with the baby's father.

"Do you still want to get married?"

"I don't think so, not right now."

"If you want to still, we will."

"No, not yet."

"Okay, whatever you want. I still love you, you know?"

"Yes, I know."

Finally my tears came. Thank you, God, for the tears, the grief, and the sadness. No more was there no feeling.

*

This time, when I thought back over the fifteen years, it started out in the usual way—a story that happened to someone I knew. When I started writing, though, the words became more of my history than they ever had before. Rather than separating my thinking and feeling, I connected them. I made discoveries.

Now when I think and feel, the word *miscarriage* isn't as awkward and my guilt is gone. I know more of myself and realize that if I could have set everything down and adjusted to carry things all the way, I would have.

Now when I think and feel, the sadness of the memory tells me I am more than simply a number in the statistic of "one in five." I am a caring woman, an almost-mother, who occasionally wonders about the possible, potential, almost-child.

Mostly now when I think and feel, I am proud of the strength that is still in me. The strength I used to deal with the pain, hear the doctor's news, and make my adult decision didn't leave me forever at my father's voice. It came back, stayed, and has been with me now for fifteen years. It is growing up beautifully and I am happy for what it has added to my life.

SECOND BABY, MAYBE

Jorie Miller

That was the year you said you didn't want a baby anymore and I said I did and you said, *So I'm just supposed to hop to now and want a baby, too.* And I said, *Yes, you are. I'm sure this time. I'm not changing my mind.* And you laid on your back against peach-colored pillowcases, the light on the bedstand stood guard over the clock radio you'd already set for 6:05 in the morning. We'd spent a lot of money on a car that week and the war had just broken out. It was snowy and cold. Everywhere we went we pulled our scarves up against the bitter wind. You could have sulked a long time, but then you wouldn't get what you wanted anyway, which was another child, and you wouldn't get sex either. It was already after ten. Within two weeks I was pregnant. You wouldn't believe it at first, but it happened just like that. But spring came and we didn't know that as the sap began to run in the trees what stirred inside me died, then passed soft as fresh liver from my body. Flowers rose from the ground and could have made me angry, but all I wanted was flowers. Send carnations, mums, birds of paradise flaunting their purple tongues. In a downpour you planted a tree as if your life depended on it, its branches symmetrical as the strings of a harp. You dug a hole. At its bottom you placed the tree, then a white handkerchief that held the red seed we would have called daughter or son, then the dirt. Rain dripped from your jacket hood, onto your nose, drops rolled down your face. In the summer we tried again. Set no morning alarms. The sun came up early and went down late. In the heat, new life took hold.

THE LACEMAKERS: A HEALING METAPHOR

Freda Curchack Marver

For years, I've lived under the delusion that ours is a family of four: a father, a mother, a daughter, and a yet-to-be-born child. I winced when people referred to Denise as an only child because I didn't see her that way; to me she was a child whose sibling was coming. Now, I'm reshaping that image. My family is the three of us, and I need to celebrate what we have.

For the past eight years, I focused my energy on trying to have a baby. This included operations on both my husband and me, nearly twenty inseminations, two cycles of in vitro fertilization and two miscarriages. A few months ago, we made the decision to stop infertility treatment. I have spent those months mourning my loss. While I am not over this mourning period, I am moving on. Denise is ten and her childhood is more than half over. My daughter and I need to make the most of the years we have left.

This summer, at Denise's request, we went to a craft fair. It was early in the summer, when it still feels exciting to go outdoors without a sweater. The fair was outside on a big grassy knoll. We held hands, swung our arms, and sang a silly song as we sauntered from booth to booth. Denise and I oohed and aahed over what was for sale, realizing where our tastes were different and where they were the same. We ran off in opposite directions in search of treasures, calling out to each other, "Mom, did you see this?" and "Denise, I found something you'll love!" There were paper sculpture wall hangings and ornate leather bags. Delicate, dangling earrings and wild, funky jewelry. Handmade felt hats. Whimsical mirrors with faces and feathers. Chairs that hung from the ceiling. Lamp bases that looked like sculptures. Clocks made out of buttons and bottle caps.

Many flashy exhibits caught my eye that day, but the one that struck me the most was not flashy at all. From a distance, I noticed two women sitting quietly, side by side, looking down at a table, doing something with their hands. As I approached, I saw them skillfully choosing between a confusing tangle of a hundred pieces of thread. It took me a moment to realize what they were doing: making lace.

I'd never seen lace being made. For me, this would be painstaking. I don't have the patience or manual dexterity to sit for hours picking two pieces of thread, tying them in a knot, putting them down; picking another two pieces, twisting them together, putting them down; picking another two pieces, knotting them, and putting them down. The repetition makes me cringe. I can't embroider. I hate to sew. A friend once taught me to knit and I was so tense and clumsy that we laughed at the thought of knitting ever being a relaxing activity for me. Forget fine motor coordination. Give me a dance floor. Let me kick my legs and swing my arms. But don't ever make me sit so still, moving only my fingers.

Yet, here were these women. When I looked at their fingers and followed the threads back to their beginnings, I saw intricately patterned lace growing out of the tangled threads. I thought about asking the women how long it had taken to make those tiny pieces, but I didn't even want to know. Making lace is not defined by the time it takes to create, but by the process itself, and the beautiful, delicate patterns that emerge.

Denise and I stayed with the lacemakers until we got fidgety watching them work so intensely, so slowly, so carefully. As we left their booth, I spread my fingers and vigorously shook my hands, flicking my wrists as though shaking down a thermometer. Watching the lacemakers made me that tense, and haunted me, too.

*

Months later, I went on a healing retreat. We talked not only of healing the body, but of healing the spirit. At that retreat, I thought about my infertility and miscarriages, where I've been and where I need to go. Consciously sorting through my life in a way I hadn't before, I realized I had already taken several steps along my healing journey.

My marriage is still intact—no small feat, given the fact that many couples are torn apart by infertility. I have a relationship with my daughter that I celebrate. It is getting easier to be around pregnant women and little children. I can talk about my miscarriages and infertility experiences without getting as upset as I did in the past. I am preparing for my future, realizing that what lies ahead is not delivering a baby, but perhaps developing a new career. I am also making plans for our family of three, thinking of travels that would not have been possible with an infant. Importantly, I am becoming aware of the supportive community around me. For many years, I went through the trauma of infertility virtually alone. I have become more open in seeking the support of others, and when I looked for support, I found it.

Of course, there are still loose ends. We have not decided whether we will pursue adoption. I'm not over the anger and grief. Sometimes situations arise that trigger deep and painful memories, tears and jealousies; I do not know when, if ever, I will be free of these. I need a ritual—a ceremony or symbolic action—to publicly acknowledge the loss of my dream and to gather support to move on. I know my healing is not complete because I am not ready to give away Denise's old baby clothes, her toys, and my maternity dresses.

For years, I have sought, without success, a healing metaphor—an image I could conjure up when the pain of infertility and miscarriage overwhelmed me. As tears formed or bitterness gripped my gut, I wanted to picture a charm. By focusing on that charm, my anger and grief could melt away. The image would be a shortcut: I wouldn't have to deal with my entangled emotions and history. Just the image itself would force the vise open, loosen the grip.

As I sifted through my thoughts at that healing retreat, I tried to envision a way to symbolize my progress, to remind myself of how far I'd come. I thought of all the loose ends from my infertility and miscarriages: those picked up and resolved, and those which I hadn't even touched.

Suddenly I thought of the lacemakers and their tedious process of sorting through the threads. This is exactly what my healing process entails: seeing many loose threads before me, deciding which to pick up, which to deal with, which to tie up in a knot of resolution and then put down, let go. The process is repeated over and over again. It is not easy and it takes a long time.

The lacemakers define their accomplishment by the tangible, beautiful lace they create. I cannot see my handiwork, but want to feel that my loose ends are being resolved in some form or pattern. I want to be able to look back and say, "Look what I have done. Look what I have made." The more ends I tie up, the larger my piece of lace will be.

Yet lace is defined not by its threads, but by its spaces. Because of the holes, lovely patterns emerge. It is comforting to know that even as I tie up loose ends, the finished product must have holes. In fact, those very holes define the essence of the work.

Infertility has left a gaping hole in my life, but it is not the infertility that creates the holes in my lace. The grief of infertility has not brought beauty to my life. Instead, I believe that my healing journey is helping me break down the magnitude of my loss into manageable pieces, and as I work around them, I am creating something beautiful: the delicate, ongoing fabric of my life.

It is not just the lace that I am learning to appreciate, but the process of making it. One of the women at the fair held her threads in place with ordinary straight pins stuck in a board. The other woman decorated her straight pins with beautiful beads. Some were stunningly bright colors, some were opaque, and others sparkled and let light through. I commented to her that the beaded pins with the taut strings attached to them looked like a piece of art itself. She replied that the beaded pins were wonderful because as she moved them around, the beads fell into ever-changing and exquisite patterns.

I need to find my own beads, the gems in my life that give the process weight, help me along my way, and provide beauty. My gems are the people in my life: my husband, my daughter, and my community of friends and family. They give me bearing—a sense of where I am, brightening and lightening my way.

I love the lace metaphor. Not only is it helping me heal, it reminds me of the wonderful afternoon Denise and I spent together on the grassy knoll at the fair. It celebrates our relationship as mother and daughter.

After a loss, we are often told to cherish what we have. The irony of my infertility and miscarriage is this: I cherish exactly what I lack. The more I treasure my daughter, the more acutely I feel the pain of not having more children. Joy and grief melt into one, consuming me. But now, I have a new way to comfort myself as I travel in my healing. I close my eyes, breathe deeply, and in the darkness, I see a painfully small, poignantly delicate, ever-growing piece of lace.

PART OF A CONVERSATION WITH DEATH

Shelley Getten

And then you reached inside
and snatched the baby growing in my womb.
I felt your icy fingers pull her away.
She, who hadn't breathed the air
or known how much
we would have loved her.
Love's as meaningless to you
as life itself, though without life
you could not be, oh arbitrary Death,
no one can destroy you.

I know we are helpless
against your cold, bony claw coming down—
a giant hook across the stage,
but I will never forgive you,
never give you anyone again
without a fight.

THE STONES OF CHILDREN

Rachel Faldet

There have been children from our house who have died and some are buried on the top of the hill. An overgrown carriage road through our backyard woods used to take people to that cemetery. Now poison ivy, goldenrod, and sumac edge this foot-path. Wild grape vines and virginia creeper wind around the basswood trees. Maples are heavy with leaves that are beginning to turn to the colors that mark their deaths. My husband, daughter, and I walk carefully as blackberry vines try to catch us. On this September afternoon we are going to the cemetery to look for little Kissie Landers, who wants to be an angel.

I have no family buried in the cemetery above our house, but wherever I've lived I've always walked the cemeteries looking for the old stones: white marble shaped into thin tablets whose words are partially covered with lichens, dark granite stones with carved hands folded in rest, white zinc markers inscribed "Gone But Not Forgotten." Even before I could read engraved names and dates, I played in the cemetery behind my parents' house, a church parsonage.

Until I was eight, I lived in a village where the people were old. Slope-backed women twisted their white hair in long braids around their heads and pinned coils in place with tortoiseshell combs. Frail men talked of coming to America from Norway when they were boys and said they'd made the right decision to farm new soil. But it would be good, they thought, if they could see their people back home one last time.

Selmer Peterson took care of the cemetery in that village. He mowed around the gravestones and trimmed what he'd missed with sharp clippers he kept in a gray shed under a windbreak of pines. He watered geraniums and blue forget-me-nots and threw away plastic flowers faded from too much sun. Even if I'd been playing alone in the cemetery earlier in the day—conducting a funeral for a doll who'd been ill or resting my back against a gravestone after I'd picked purple violets from a section where no one was buried—I'd go down again if Selmer was working.

Sometimes as I followed him in his work, he told me about the people buried there—they were his friends, friends of his family, his family. I knew where Knut Peterson and his wife Kristina were. I knew the Jorgensons were a few stones down. I knew where the children were. There were more children in the cemetery than in the village. Knowing they died of influenza as three-year-olds or from complications a few days after their births didn't scare me, though I would never walk over their graves. I'd walk around them, in case they had open eyes and could see me, or could feel my weight on their bodies. The children were all together, Selmer said, because when a child dies it breaks your heart.

My daughter Elizabeth is five years old. David and I started taking her on walks to the cemetery a few years ago when we moved to our home, a brick gothic revival house built in the 1860's. At the south end of the cemetery by the Hansens and Bullocks is a gazebo Elizabeth calls her summer house. That is always her first destination after we've left the footpath. David usually keeps walking, but Elizabeth and I often sit in this place under a canopy of pines. Sometimes I tell her a story; sometimes she sings a song while we rest. Then we get up and go to nearby stones of people we feel we know because we've looked at them many times. She helps me find the old stones, with vines twining up to heaven, with hands shaking in farewell, with lambs kneeling on white marble.

"Who lives here?" Elizabeth asks when she sees an upright stone that she's not noticed before.

I read, "Hannah Patre, wife of Silas Patre." Elizabeth wonders, "How old is she?"

"Twenty-nine," I answer. Numbers don't mean much to her yet. Twenty-nine and ninety-nine are the same in her mind.

"Twenty-nine is old," she tells me.

Next to Hannah Patre's marker is a small flat stone, sinking into the ground. It says, "Baby." Hannah Patre died in childbirth, I think as Elizabeth runs to David. I could have died in childbirth. I would have died if I had had my daughter one hundred years earlier. I would have bled to death. No doctor or neighbor woman could have saved my life. This would be my grave of weeping willows.

When I was ten, after I'd moved from the village to a larger town, my friend Mary Elise and I would walk to the cemetery and look for the little Kittleson girls. They all died on the same day. They'd been playing in a quarry, but weren't supposed to be. By dusk the sisters were lost until someone saw a shoe sticking out of a heap of crushed rock. "Here they are," Mary Elise would shout if she found them first. I would run over and we would stand together reading their markers. It could have been us, we thought, but never said out loud.

"Mom, come on. Dad and I are waiting," Elizabeth calls from a few rows away. "We've found Kissie."

"I'm coming," I answer, though I walk slowly. I am looking for graves of infants—children who couldn't yet pronounce their names, children just learning to walk, children who died close to their births.

Sophia Jacobsen was born on September 28, 1876, and died on November 28, 1877. Edith Lee died June 10, 1877, aged 2 months and 12 days. Her sister, Ada, died before her, November 23, 1875, aged 1 year, 2 months, and 16 days. Their white zinc stone is inscribed, "Children of W.W. and P.C. Lee, Our Darlings, They Sweetly Sleep."

As I go from row to row in this old section, I try to catalog these children so that later I can remember their names and their short lives. I imagine them being brought up the carriage road in a hearse, with fringed black drapes covering the long glass panes on each side, pulled by a team of coal black, matched horses. I imagine their small caskets being lowered into the ground and covered with dirt. I imagine their mothers, wearing long black mourning dresses and veiled hats, coming to these places and standing where I stand.

I have no place to stand. The two I lost were not even born. They were thrown away with the blood. They were too young to ask for. They have no names.

Abigail Rose Sorenson. Lara Sadie Jensen. William Winneshiek York. Nellie Mae Peck. Charlie. Little Margaret. Our Jimmie. Dearest Nels. Our Darling. Baby.

"Here she is," says Elizabeth as I walk closer. David has already read the stone to her and he has walked on. Elizabeth rubs her hand over the arch of Kissie's marker. It is just Elizabeth's height. In a circle near the top of the stone is a carved angel, her body curved as if floating and her hands folded over her chest. Underneath are the words, "I want to be an angel." Kissie was 10 years, 5 months, and 13 days old. She died November 10, 1862, and was the daughter of E.B. and S.W. Landers.

"Why did she want to be an angel instead of a little girl?" my daughter asks.

As a little girl I was once an angel. My mother draped a cotton sheet around me and secured it with a belt of silver garland. She bent black coat hangers and covered them with white tissue paper and fastened them to my shoulders. She bobby-pinned a halo of tinsel to my head. I guarded the baby Jesus, a plastic doll in a receiving blanket, as his earthly mother sat by his manger at the front of the church while the congregation sang *Silent Night*. Later that evening as I walked home through the December snow with my parents and brother and sister, my wings in my hands, I thought, "We're happy now, but baby Jesus was born to die. His mother's heart will break in the spring."

"Kissie's parents were so sad about her death," I answer Elizabeth, "that they thought of their little girl as an angel in heaven. That comforted them. I don't think Kissie really wanted to be one so soon. She probably wanted to live longer with her family."

I'm not sure if it is better to have known your children—fed them, whispered stories to them, held them close to your heart—before you lose them or if it is better to know them unborn before they die. You can publicly mourn someone others have met, someone people were expecting, someone who looks like a child. I mourn children who most people never knew about, never expected, who never looked like children.

"If I wanted to be an angel, would I die?" Elizabeth asks.

"Wanting to be one won't make you die," I answer. "You can pretend you are one."

Elizabeth runs past a marker—perhaps belonging to Kissie's aunt—cast into the shape of a tree trunk. On one side is an artist's palette and the words "God Knows Best" and on another is a tipped flower pot with a vine of twisted leaves. Elizabeth wants to see Nellie Mae Peck whose name is inscribed on the marble base of a kneeling cherub.

"I'm going to Dad," she says after she strokes the cherub's head.

I walk slowly. Reading names of children whose mothers, too, have long ago died, I am not so alone in my quiet grief.

Frankie. Dear Little Ferdy. Lily. Josiah.

My great-grandmother had a child who died, but no one seems to know how old the baby was. My grandfather, an only child, says he remembers hearing about a boy, but doesn't know if he was born before or after him. He doesn't know if the baby was miscarried, a stillbirth, or an infant death. No one mentions this child, but I ask. I only know about this because when I was twelve my mother let me choose between two rings she kept in a velvet box in her dresser drawer: a circle of emeralds with a pearl in the center or a crown of opals and diamond chips. I took the opal ring, the ring that my great-grandfather gave my great-grandmother after she lost the baby.

I have lost two babies. I lost each of these children at the end of their first trimesters. They would have been Elizabeth's younger brothers or sisters. They would have had names. They would have been with us as we walk through the cemetery above our house. They would have been part of our family.

When I walk this cemetery I feel connected to the families who've lived in our house before us. To piece together these people's lives, my husband read fragile documents in the courthouse, newspaper articles preserved on microfilm, and county histories printed on thick ivoried paper. The man who built our house followed the frontier and is buried out West, but many of the others who lived in our house are buried here.

The Traceys are in a cluster around a thick stone that names the family. The parents, Alva and Phebe, died as old people in our house in the 1890's. Their sons, Horace and Homer, died 3 days apart of scarlet fever. Horace died on July 7, 1875, at age 27 years, 5 months, and 13 days. Homer was 20 years, 6 months, and 16 days. They are buried side by side. Alva and Phebe's granddaughter, Ade, died in March of 1887 at age 2 years, 1 month, and 4 days. In a county history her death is recorded as one of the year's tragedies: she sat down in a bucket of scalding water. Often we look for their graves on our walks. On this September day, though, I stay near the infants, the very young children, and little Kissie Landers.

Kissie Landers. Abigail Rose Sorenson. Lara Sadie Jensen. William Winneshiek York. Nellie Mae Peck. Charlie. Little Margaret. Our Jimmie. Dearest Nels. Our Darling. Baby. My December Baby. My September Baby.

"Let's go home," I hear Elizabeth say as she runs toward me. She and David have watered the geraniums and vinca in the folk-art planter decorated with china shards, glass pieces, and marbles that mark his grandparents' plots. "We're done. I want to go back to our house," she yells to urge me to come.

David and Elizabeth want to go home by way of the overgrown footpath, but I cannot retrace my way through the cemetery past the children to get there again. I do not want to undo the comfort the old stones have given me. "The woods are in too much of a tangle," I say to them. "Let's go the other way." We join hands and walk down the curved road to the main entrance, taking the long way back to our house, which has lost many of its children, known and unknown, named and unnamed.

CODA: A JOURNAL ENTRY ONE YEAR LATER

Altha Edgren

I am thinking about the baby at this the one-year anniversary of her passing. About the ultrasound, about seeing her beautiful face, about the doctor telling us she had no chance of survival.

About her leaving me, about all of the women who comforted me with stories of their lost babies, a sorority of sorrow, these women, and now myself among them, moving past the pain to find a jagged peace in comforting another suffering sister.

ABOUT THE CONTRIBUTORS

Rebecca D. Anthony wrote her poem after watching her present husband playing with her three children from her previous marriage. She wondered how he must have felt after losing two of their own. They now have four children—two girls and two boys. After living in Illinois for nine years, they are returning to their native Colorado to finish raising their children among family.

Susan J. Berkson is a writer and broadcast commentator whose columns appear in the *Minneapolis Star Tribune* and *Minnesota Women's Press*. She often writes on politics and gender. She holds degrees from Macalester College and the University of Minnesota. Her work has appeared in various newspapers and magazines, as well as on public radio and public television.

Karen Chakoian is a minister at Central Presbyterian Church in Des Moines, Iowa where she lives with her husband and son, Benjamin. She is an Illinois native but has been in Des Moines for over a decade. Karen likes to read, garden, and spend time with family and friends. Her essay is adapted from a sermon she wrote.

Faye Ann Chappell is a substitute teacher and tutor from Pittsboro, Indiana. She enjoys reading, writing, home decorating, and outdoor activities. She and her husband are active in their church and its school. They have one daughter, Alicia.

Deborah L. Cooper is a full-time mother of two children, Evan and Tess, who was born several years after Deborah wrote in her journal about her miscarriage. Deborah was born and raised on a farm in north-central Iowa. Tending flowers on a city lot that is one-third of an acre is her passion and stress eliminator. Her seven-year-old son calls her a "garden mother."

Betty Davids lives in Buffalo Center, Iowa with her husband, John III. They have four children: Jill, Heather, Courtney, and John IV. Betty operates an antiques and collectibles shop, and is the area newscaster on 107.3 KIOW every weekday morning. She enjoys reading and listening to music.

Amy Desherlia lives in Cottage Hills, Illinois and works as a teacher's assistant at Toddle Towne Learning Center. She enjoys spending time with her boyfriend, Jeff, and her family, including her niece and nephew.

Altha Edgren works as a medical writer and plays as a poet and novelist. She lives near the St. Croix River Valley in Minnesota with her two children, Kira and Kyle; two cats; and two hamsters.

Deborah Edwards is a nutritionist for residents of nursing homes and children with special needs. During the 1994-95 academic year, Deborah and her husband were co-directors of the Luther College study abroad program in Nottingham, England. While she has published professionally, this is Deborah's first published personal essay. She enjoys the outdoors, traveling, volunteering, and being with friends and family.

Sarah Entenmann and her husband live in rural Northfield, Minnesota where she grows petunias, chives, and dandelions. They have two children, Leah and David. Sarah is the promotion director of 89.3 WCAL, the public radio service of St. Olaf College. Writing gives voice to some of her deepest emotions; she wishes she had more time for it.

Evelyn Fielding lives in Mankato, Minnesota and is a prolific writer of poetry. Her poems have appeared in *Blueberry Pie* and *Collections of Poems for the Unknown Child*.

Nancy Fitzgerald teaches creative writing and is co-chair of Women's Studies at the College of St. Scholastica in Duluth, Minnesota. She has published many poems and has a chapbook titled *An Inward Turning Out*. With child raising completed, she lives with her husband and their Airedale pup.

Donna S. Frary holds a master's degree in adult continuing education. She recently made a career change from a university residence hall director to a legislative aide/office coordinator for an Illinois state representative. She enjoys living in a quiet house after residing in a dormitory for seven years. Donna likes to read, garden, bike, and listen to music in her spare time.

Susan Geise is a West Virginia native. She is a social worker who directs the Pain Management Program at Good Shepherd Rehabilitation Hospital in Allentown, Pennsylvania. She has a private practice in counseling with Bell Labs. She and her husband, Russell, have two children, Natalie and Audrey. She enjoys jazz dancing, gardening, and keeping in tune with family and friends.

Shelley Getten is a Minnesota native, residing near Minneapolis with her husband, Brien, and two children, Devin and Brighid. She is a part-time banquet waitress but her first job is raising her children to be loving and conscientious adults. She belongs to several writing groups and has recently been published in various journals and anthologies.

Lisa A. Harlan is working toward an interdisciplinary degree in humanities, communication, and management. She is a buyer for Warn Industries in Milwaukie, Oregon. In her leisure time she likes to bake, read novels, write, and remodel her house. She is the mother of one daughter, Kelsey.

Mary Lynn Hill lives in Des Moines, Iowa and has been a nurse clinician working with cancer patients for fifteen years. The mother of two children, she is active in environmental groups and the American Cancer Society. She enjoys camping, biking, and traveling.

Stuart Johnston lives in Decorah, Iowa and has worked at Luther College in the Student Life Office for a decade. He and his wife, Carol, have one daughter, Katie. He enjoys running, biking, snow-shoeing, cross-country skiing, and reading.

Dianne H. Kobberdahl, an Iowa native, works as an occupational therapist for Iowa Health Systems in Des Moines, Iowa. She holds a master's degree from Rush University. Her interests include freelance writing, walking, health issues, and music. Dianne and her husband, Steve, have one son, Jacob.

Keith Kuenning is a graduate student pursuing a Ph.D. in United States diplomatic history. He and his wife, Tess, have two children, Gerard and Anne. It took five pregnancies to bring their two children into the world. Keith believes it is important to have courage to keep trying after a miscarriage.

Angela LaFisca is a Shreveport, Louisiana native. Angela and her husband recently built a log house. After three miscarriages, she gave birth to Elizabeth Nicole on February 14, 1996. Angela works as a secretary, loves to sing, and is active in her church.

Jay Lake was born and raised overseas. He now speaks nationally on Internet marketing, creates and implements interactive marketing communications strategies, writes science fiction, and develops software. He and his wife, Susan, live, still childless, in an older home in Austin, Texas.

Beth Lamsam works and lives in Des Moines, Iowa. She and her husband, Jesse, have two children, Amelia and Joseph.

Kathy Law lives in the country near Churdan, Iowa. She and her husband, Dave, farm and operate a craft business. They have one son, Jonathan. Kathy enjoys making crafts, teaching Sunday school at her church, and being a Cub Scout leader.

LaDawna Lawton is from Lemoore, California and has been a volunteer with Sharing Parents (a support group for parents whose babies have died) for over four years. Family is top priority for LaDawna and her husband, Steve. LaDawna stays home with their children, Kaitlen and Brian, who was born several months after LaDawna wrote her essay.

Roseann Lloyd has published several books of poetry and nonfiction. Her latest book, *War Baby Express*, is a collection of poems that explores women's issues that are often invisible in American culture. About her poem, "Tribe," Roseann says that the real anthropologist was disturbed about her job description—excavating burial sites—and left her position shortly after seeing the grave of a child. Roseann conducts poetry workshops and lives in Minnesota.

Natalie Magruder recently completed a nursing degree and is working as a registered nurse at a plasma donor center. Several months before completing her degree, she and her husband welcomed the birth of Chase Michael.

Karen Martin-Schramm is the administrative assistant to the president of Luther College in Decorah, Iowa. She and her husband, Jim, have two children, Joel and Joshua.

Freda Curchack Marver writes and conducts workshops on dreams, loss, and healing. She is writing a book that asks: what happens to faith when prayers don't come true? Freda lives in Minneapolis, Minnesota with her husband, daughter, and dog. She enjoys being with friends, dancing, solving crossword puzzles, and eating at restaurants that make exquisite dishes she would never attempt on her own.

Jon Masson holds a master's degree in journalism from Drake University. He is a sportswriter for the *La Crosse Tribune*. Previously he worked as a journalist for *The Phoenix Gazette* and *Colorado Springs Sun*. Jon and his wife, Patrice, live in Onalaska, Wisconsin.

Jan Mathew lives in Lafayette, Indiana with her husband, daughter, and son. She is employed as managing editor of the *Lafayette Leader*, a weekly community newspaper. She enjoys reading, running, and frequent freelance writing projects.

Deborah McCleary and her husband, David, live in Allentown, Pennsylvania with their two sons, Christopher and Trevor. Deborah ended her career as a certified public accountant when she went on bedrest during her pregnancy with their first living child, Christopher. She is active in church activities and likes to swim, needlepoint, and read.

Jorie Miller has a master's degree in creative writing from the University of Minnesota. She has published poetry in a number of journals, including *Mothering, North Coast Review*, and *Rag Mag*. She has been writing and teaching in Minnesota for the past ten years, though she is now living in Belgium with her husband and two young children.

Jean Streufert Patrick lives near Mitchell, South Dakota where she is raising three children and working at her husband's veterinary clinic. While her family sleeps, she works as a freelance writer and book reviewer.

Sherri Rickabaugh is a native Iowan, living in Carlisle, Iowa. She has worked as a nurse and is now working in clinical cancer research. Sherri is an American Cancer Society volunteer and recently started volunteering at the local zoo. Her hobbies include herbal gardening and basket weaving.

Clare Rossini, a Minnesota native, is a graduate of the University of Iowa Writers' Workshop, where she was a Teaching Writing Fellow. She received her Ph.D. in American literature from Columbia University. Her poems have appeared in many journals. Clare teaches and directs the college writing program at Carleton College in Northfield, Minnesota where she lives with her husband, Joseph Byrne.

Barbara Santucci is a children's author and artist who works in a variety of mediums. She has published stories, poems, and crafts in several children's magazines. Before embarking on a colorful journey of words, paints, and pastels, she taught on both elementary and preschool levels. She is working on a B.F.A. from Northern Illinois University. She lives with her husband, Michael, and their two daughters in Belvidere, Illinois.

Terry Schock is a county social worker and has lived in Des Moines, Iowa her whole life. Her professional interest involves being a children's advocate. She and her husband, Bob, enjoy traveling and have been to Europe twice, with the hope of traveling to Egypt in the future. She is also a member of a dance troupe. Terry and her husband have a son, Mike.

Emily Martha Schultz, a psychologist, lives in Natick, Massachusetts with her husband, son, and daughter. Her daughter was born nine months after the completion of her essay. She maintains a psychotherapy practice, and also performs psychological evaluations for the courts.

Carla Sofka is an assistant professor in the School of Social Welfare, University of Albany. Although her clinical work and research focus on grief and loss, she reports that her miscarriage has been her most profound learning experience. Since moving to New York from Illinois, she enjoys spending time exploring the area with her husband, Mike, and her dog.

Cindy Steines and her husband, Merl, operate an organic dairy goat farm in rural Decorah, Iowa. She enjoys gardening and music. This is her first published essay.

Dylan Ann Treall and her husband, Les, live in a supportive co-housing community in Seattle, Washington. Before the birth of their daughter in December 1995, Dylan began instruction in the art of healing through energy work. Her area of interest is the birth process. She is working toward a bachelor's degree in prenatal and perinatal psychology and hopes to serve as a labor support person.

Deborah Vaughan is a secondary English teacher at Washington High School in Vinton, Iowa. Her second job is at home where she tends to husband Milton of nearly twenty years and Dylan Thomas, their young son. She likes reading to Dylan and reveling in his ever-increasing imagination. In her spare time she reads and writes for herself.

Jan Wagener resides in Minneapolis, Minnesota with partner, Patrick, and two children. She works outside her home as a probation officer. She has written poetry for years but only recently has had the courage to be published. Her work has appeared in *Gypsy Cab* and *Sidewalks*.

Anne Walters and her husband, Mike, live and work in Decorah, Iowa. She enjoys reading, gardening, cooking, and taking care of her two dogs. Anne has been published in *The New Oneota Review*.

Lori Watts lives in Lawton, Iowa with her husband, Scott, and their two children, Amy and Adam. Lori has been a nurse but now has elected to stay home with the children. She volunteers at the HEARTS (Helping Empty Arms Recover Through Sharing) support program whenever she can.

Kelly Winters is a Wisconsin native, currently living and writing in North Carolina. She loves to travel, camp, and backpack.

Robin Worgan is a native of Philadelphia and has recently moved to Pittsburgh with her husband, Glenn, and daughter, Elizabeth. She is a full-time mother. She likes to read, skate, practice yoga, and do some late night writing. Robin's journal excerpt is her first published piece.

ABOUT THE EDITORS

Rachel Faldet is an English instructor at Luther College in Decorah, Iowa where she teaches writing classes for first-year American and international students. She received her master's degree in expository writing from the University of Iowa. Rachel is a freelance writer and editor; some of her essays have appeared in *Iowa Woman* and *Wapsipinicon Almanac*. She recently edited *The Provocative Professor: The Billy Sihler Stories*, which was published by Luther College. Rachel and her husband, David, are the parents of two children, Elizabeth and Pearl. Now that this quilt of words, *Our Stories of Miscarriage*, has left her upstairs workspace, Rachel is making a quilt of cottons for each of her daughters. She has had two miscarriages.

Karen Fitton lives in a one-hundred-year-old house in Decorah, Iowa with her husband, Robert, and their two children, Reed and Jenna. She earned her bachelor of science degree in biology from Western Illinois University. Karen has kept a journal for twenty-five years and writes poetry for herself. When she is not helping Robert with house restoration, Karen divides her time between family, four cats, creating fabric designs using ancient Japanese techniques, her freelance sewing business, and volunteer work. Karen had a miscarriage before the birth of her son, Reed.

RESOURCES

National Organizations Concerned with Miscarriage

Bereavement Services/RTS
Gundersen Lutheran Medical Center
1910 South Avenue
La Crosse, Wisconsin 54601
Phone (608) 791-4747 or (800) 362-9567, ext. 4747

The Compassionate Friends, Inc.
National Office
P.O. Box 3696
Oak Brook, Illinois 60522-3696
Phone (708) 990-0010

Pregnancy and Infant Loss Center
1421 East Wayzata Boulevard, Suite 30
Wayzata, Minnesota 55391
Phone (612) 473-9372

RESOLVE, Inc.
1310 Broadway
Somerville, Massachusetts 02144-1731
Phone (617) 623-0744

National SHARE Office
St. Joseph's Health Center
300 First Capitol Drive
St. Charles, Missouri 63301-2893
Phone (314) 947-6164 or (800) 821-6819

Allen, Marie, and Shelly Marks. *Miscarriage: Women Sharing from the Heart.* New York: John Wiley and Sons, 1993.

Davis, Deborah L. *Empty Cradle, Broken Heart: Surviving the Death of Your Baby.* Golden, Colorado: Fulcrum Publishing, 1991.

Hanson, Michelle Fryer. *Infertility: The Emotional Journey.* Minneapolis: Deaconess Press, 1994.

Harkness, Carla. *The Infertility Book: A Comprehensive Medical and Emotional Guide.* Berkeley: Celestial Arts Publishing, 1992.

Kohn, Ingrid, and Perry-Lynn Moffitt. *A Silent Sorrow: Pregnancy Loss: Guidance and Support for You and Your Family.* New York: Dell Publishing, 1992.

Limbo, Rana K., and Sara Rich Wheeler. *When a Baby Dies: A Handbook for Healing and Helping.* La Crosse, Wisconsin: Resolve Through Sharing, 1986.

924277